That Patchwork Place

Crazy Rags

Deborah Brunner

That Patchwork Place®

Credits

Editor-in-Chief	Kerry I. Hoffman
Managing Editor	Judy Petry
Technical Editor	Barbara Weiland
Design Director	Kay Green
Copy Editors	Liz McGehee
	Sherri Schultz
Proofreader	Melissa Riesland
Illustrator	Brian Metz
Illustration Assistant	Bruce Stout
Photographer	Brent Kane
Text and Cover Designer	Cheryl Stevenson
Production Assistant	Shean Bemis

Crazy Rags: Contemporary Wearable Art
© 1996 by Deborah Brunner
That Patchwork Place, Inc., PO Box 118
Bothell, WA 98041-0118 USA

Printed in the United States of America
01 00 99 98 97 96   6 5 4 3 2 1

Library of Congress Cataloging-in-Publication Data
Brunner, Deborah,
    Crazy rags : contemporary wearable art / by
Deborah Brunner.
      p. cm.
    ISBN 1-56477-166-0
    1. Coats. 2. Vests. 3. Quilting—Patterns.
4. Quilted goods. 5. Wearable art. I. Title.
TT535.B78 1996
746.46'0432—dc20   96-21629
                                                          CIP

Dedication

To my husband, Tom, for all the love and support you have given me, and to the memory of my grandmother, Reah Elizabeth Horstman. I know you are watching over me.

Acknowledgments

Thank you to all the friends who have made this book possible:
My mother, Janice Martin, who gave me my first pieces of fabric;
Beth Donaldson, who prodded me into a teaching career;
The rest of the "Outlaws," Rhonda Anderson, Diedra Garlock, and Karen Mirras, for their encouragement and support and the fabulous garments they provided for this book;
Laurie Gass, former owner of Quilting Memories in Bath, Michigan, who gave me her friendship and a fabulous place to teach;
Capital City Quilt Guild members, for all the wonderful years of sharing and inspiration;
Enola Clegg and Maria Lopez, for my introduction to crazy quilting;
Katy and Colleen Donaldson, along with their mom, Beth, for the beautiful vests;
Maureen Carlson and Melody Naskale, for the wonderful jackets done in record time; and
My students, for their inspiration and enthusiasm.
A special thank-you to the wonderful people at That Patchwork Place: Kerry Hoffman for her belief in my idea; Barbara Weiland, for her humor, expertise, and unfailing suport of this project; Brent Kane, whose photography brought the garments to life and kept me breathing all the while; Cheryl Stevenson, who put all the elements together with such style; and the entire family at That Patchwork Place, for making my vision a reality.

Table of Contents

Introduction

I have been enamored of fabric since I was very young. I was lucky enough to have a grandmother who was a seamstress and a mother who sewed too. I started sewing at the age of nine, first for my Barbie® doll and then, as I grew older, for myself. Over the years, I have continued to sew clothing, at times out of necessity, but more often for the pleasure of having a unique garment.

When I began to quilt in the mid-1980s, my passion for fabric reached a new level. I could actually collect fabric without feeling I had to use it immediately! In my quest for fabrics to add to my growing stash, I also discovered many other interesting decorative embellishments to collect.

This book was born out of my passion for (really my addiction to) collecting fabric, buttons, beads, and embroidery findings. I am convinced this passion was passed to me genetically from my grandmother, Reah Elizabeth Horstman, who was the greatest collector of all!

As my collection grew to fill the shelves of my workroom, I was faced with the challenge of using it. Each and every scrap of fabric, every button, every bead and charm meant something to me and, of course, deserved a special showcase. When I discovered silk-ribbon embroidery and crazy quilting a few years ago, I thought about combining these techniques with the knowledge of clothing design I had developed during my previous exploration of weaving. Back then, in order to maintain the structural integrity of my handwoven fabrics as much as possible, I wove squares and rectangles, then cut garment pieces from them, trying to keep the number of cuts to a minimum. It was a challenge to work with the geometric shapes to create garments for my wardrobe.

The unit construction that I devised for my woven pieces seemed a natural format for making embellished patchwork garments, using the crazy-quilt method of piecing scraps together and adding lavish hand embroidery. My dilemma was resolved! Not only would I be able to use my collection, but the project pieces would be portable, too, and easy to make into a fashionable garment—a wearable work of art!

This book is the result of melding my desire to use my stash of goodies with my love of crazy patchwork and my weaving experience. Each garment design in this book was created by sewing together groups of squares or rectangles to make a simply styled garment—with no pattern pieces required. Careful fabric selection and embellishment resulted in the pizzazz required to turn each garment shape into a unique piece of wearable art. It has been very satisfying to use many of the wonderful things I have collected over the years, as well as the new things I seem to find daily.

You are limited only by your imagination. Whether you are a novice or an experienced seamstress, I hope to spark your interest in crazy patching in the following chapters. It has been a wonderful adventure for me, and I hope you enjoy exploring my techniques and designs as much as I have enjoyed creating them.

Creating Your Wearable Work of Art

This book is meant to serve as a guide, a place to start on your own adventure with crazy patchwork. The possibilities are endless. Each of you will develop your own style in this medium. The color combinations you prefer, the type of fabrics you select, and the embroidery stitches and notions you use—each choice will play an important part in the completed vest or jacket.

If ten people were given the same fabrics and embroidery supplies to execute a particular design, each and every garment would be amazingly different. That is the best part of this concept. You can create a garment that is unique—truly one of a kind.

First, select the vest or jacket style you want to make, choosing from the six shapes featured in the projects on pages 18–65. The basic shapes are illustrated below.

Adjusting the design to fit your shape is the second step. Fitting adjustments, using my unit method of construction, are easy to make for the garment shapes in this book. Start with a vest, then move on to one of the jackets or the short coat. If you would rather start smaller and simpler, begin with the French beret (page 21) or the drawstring handbag (page 23).

Next, create the required units by crazy patching them together, then adding the embroidery—the "icing on the cake," as I like to call it. This is your opportunity to create a unique, personalized statement.

The completed crazy-patch units, ready to embroider, can be taken "on the road." Because these garments are so portable, you can stitch and embellish the completed crazy-patch units in moments snatched throughout the day. No more long waits in the doctor's office with nothing to do. Before you know it, your embroidered units will be done and ready to assemble into a fabulous garment to wear and enjoy.

So sit back, read on, and let your imagination and the suggestions in this book guide you in creating a garment that will garner rave reviews and a wonderful feeling of accomplishment.

Tuxedo Vest
(Page 48)

Mandarin Coat
(Page 26)

Safari Vest
(Page 54)

Kimono Jacket
(Page 34)

Scrappy Vest
(Page 60)

Himalayan Jacket
(Page 40)

Basic Tools and Supplies

Sewing Machine: Although you may hand piece your crazy patches together, the sewing machine is my choice because it is faster. Any straight-stitch sewing machine will do. If it is available, attach a patchwork or quilting foot designed especially for stitching accurate ¼"-wide seam allowances.

Scissors: Good, sharp scissors are very important. I recommend 8"-long bent-handled shears for cutting patches to size. You'll also need a small pair of scissors or snips to cut threads at the machine and while you are doing the embroidery stitches.

Straight Pins: You won't need pins often for the patchwork, but a slippery piece of silk may require a pin or two. You will also need them when assembling the completed units into a garment. I prefer long quilter's pins with plastic heads.

Iron and Ironing Board: If possible, position your ironing board next to your machine and lower it to table height (unless you prefer a little exercise getting up and down each time you want to press a patch).

Rotary Mat and Cutting Tools: Use these timesaving tools to cut muslin base pieces (see "Muslin" at right) for the crazy patching. My favorite is an 18" x 24" mat. I use a large rotary cutter and two rulers— a 12½" square ruler and a 5" x 24" rotary ruler.

Muslin: You will create each crazy-patch unit on a base shape cut from muslin. Choose a good-quality, 100%-cotton muslin with a permanent-press finish. Be sure to prewash it. I buy several yards at a time, then wash and dry the piece so it's ready when I get the urge to go crazy.

Sewing Thread: Use regular dressmaking thread to sew your crazy patches. You can use all those little bits left on the spools in your collection and on your bobbins to piece the patches together. By the time you're finished with the embellishing on the right side of the work, you'll never see a mismatched thread— even along a seam line.

Embroidery Threads and Needles: There is an endless variety of available supplies for embroidery. Rather than list them all here, I've included extensive information in the section on embroidery on page 71.

Fabric for Crazy Patchwork

Fabric selection is one of the most exciting aspects of crazy patchwork. It offers the opportunity to use several of your favorite fabrics in one project, as well as to try some exotic fabrics that you may never have used before. It takes only a small amount of a special fabric to add sparkle to a simple vest or jacket. Wonderful scraps from other quiltmaking and dressmaking projects often find their way into crazy patchwork, too, so think before you toss that leftover—even if it isn't very large.

Where to Shop for Fabric

There are a number of sources to consider when looking for special fabrics for crazy patchwork. Two of the obvious ones are quilt and dressmaking fabric shops.

There are so many beautiful quilting cottons available. The range of colors and patterns staggers the mind—batiks, homespun plaids, stripes, prints, solids—and more. As crazy patchwork has become more popular, many quilt shops have added specialty fabrics, such as lamé, Ultra Suede®, and velveteen, to their offerings.

You'll find other fabrics such as silks, laces, and woolens at specialty fabric shops. A fabric store I frequent has bolts piled to the ceiling and tucked wherever they have space. I was digging under a counter during a visit and ran across several bolts of imported Italian cotton from the early '50s. The tags were yellowed, but I could still see the price—a bargain by today's standards. You can be sure I bought some for my stash!

Vintage fabrics are often available at estate auctions and antique shops. They can be more costly, but a small amount of a special fabric may be just what you need for your project. Haunt garage sales for special treasures too. If you have the time, the rewards can be great. If you like the print and it's a bargain, take it home. If you are not quite sure but the price is right, take it anyway. You don't want to find yourself wishing you had bought that piece of lime green brocade you left behind because you weren't sure you would use it.

Once the word is out that you're going crazy (fabric-crazy, that is), people may bring you treasures from their attics and closets. Accept them graciously and gratefully. A friend sent me three vintage fabrics she found at a garage sale along with a note apologizing because they were blue. I rarely, if ever, use blue in my garments, but those three fabrics found their own special places in the tuxedo vest I call "Bell-Bottom Blues" (page 49). You just never know when something you wouldn't normally choose will be just right for your project.

Fabric swaps are another great way to acquire interesting fabrics you may have missed on your fabric-buying forays. Remember to buy a fabric you like when you see it; chances are you may not see it again, and the chance you will wish you had bought it is even greater.

What to Buy and How Much

For crazy patchwork, you may use fabrics made of cotton, silk, linen, rayon, or wool—or combinations of these fibers. Fabrics made of these fibers are available in a variety of weaves and textures that can add visual interest to your crazy-patchwork project. Don't overlook fabrics with metallic yarns. They add special interest to patchwork pieces. Lace and sheer fabrics are also nice additions to your work. You can layer them over other fabrics or scrunch and pleat them to add more texture.

I am an advocate of natural-fiber fabrics, in part because I am a quilter; 100% cotton fabric is the mainstay of my collection. I also use silk-ribbon embroidery on many projects. Pulling this delicate ribbon through tough synthetic fabrics can cause undue wear and tear on the silk fibers. (As interest in this type of embroidery has grown, soft flexible ribbons made from synthetics have become available; you may find that they open up a new range of possibilities.) I do use synthetic suede, such as Ultra Suede, in my work because I have found that it needles well.

If you are in doubt about fiber content or how a fabric may embroider, thread a needle with a short length of silk ribbon and try pulling it through the fabric; check for signs of wear. It takes only a few stitches to discover whether the ribbon frays—a sure sign that tough synthetic fibers (polyester or nylon) are present.

This is not to say you can't use synthetic fabrics in a crazy-patchwork project. As you make fabric selections, think of how you will use your project and the type of embroidery you want to do. Many traditional embroidery threads pass through synthetics unscathed.

My students often ask me how much to buy of a particular fabric. When I buy fabrics for destiny unknown, I purchase quarter-yard pieces. If I think the fabric may be suitable for a coordi-

nated piece of clothing or lining, I buy more. If the fabric is really special, I might buy enough to share with a friend.

How to Prepare Fabric

I wash the majority of my fabrics before I use them. I wash all cottons, linens, and rayons, and some silks. I do not recommend washing heavy, slubbed silk suiting fabrics because of unpredictable results. Silk douppioni loses its crispness when washed, so you may not want to wash it either.

I buy some fabrics (or garments made of wonderful fabrics) at garage sales and auctions. These I wash, regardless of fiber content, because I want to make sure they will hold up in the completed project. Fabrics of an indeterminate age often shred or disintegrate in the wash. I take a chance and put these fabric finds through the washing machine and the dryer on a permanent-press setting. If they come through the process intact, I add them to my fabric collection for a future project; if not, out they go!

How to Select Fabric

When selecting fabric for a particular project, I start with an inspiration fabric—one I really love or one that creates a theme—a fabric that inspires me to create my own work of art. You'll know that special piece of fabric when you see it or hear it calling, "Buy me, buy me," from the fabric-store shelf.

When selecting fabrics, I don't abide by any color rules. I think it is more important to love the fabric. When I started collecting orange and purple fabric for my Kimono Jacket (page 35), my friends did raise their eyebrows. By the time I had my squares patched and embroidered, though, they were amazed and their eyebrows were back in place.

One thing to keep in mind is that the patches you will cut to make the crazy patchwork are relatively small, so what may look bold on the bolt or in something as small as a fat quarter, will look different in your project. When scanning a printed fabric for possibilities, I often hold my hands in the pose that movie directors and art students use to view a scene or their work—thumbs together with fingers perpendicular to form a box around various sections or motifs. It helps me isolate areas that I may want to embellish and helps me see how a particular motif will look when cut away from the rest of the fabric.

After selecting the inspiration fabric, select others that coordinate with and accent it. When I am planning a garment, I often pull between twelve and twenty fabrics for the project. You will usually need a minimum of twelve fabrics. The more choices you have, the better. A scrap of this, a quarter yard of that, and you are ready to begin. Choose light and dark fabrics, prints and solids, and different textures of similar colors. Decide how much contrast you want between your patches, and remember that delicate embroidery stitches don't show up well against busy prints. I love prints, so I generally take a bold approach to my embroidery, creating a textured fabric that has become "my style." Remember that you don't need large pieces of fabrics. On occasion, I have found just the right piece of fabric in a scrap bag of old clothing. In the end, I may not use each fabric I have pulled from my stash, but the option is there should I wish to do so.

As you make your fabric selections for the current project, arrange them in a circle around the inspiration fabric to audition them—to make sure they work together. Don't be afraid to ex-periment, adding fabrics that at first glance might not seem to work. Give yourself permission to try new things without fear of failure. Remember, "Nothing ventured, nothing gained." If you have selected fabrics you love, it will all work out. It's so exciting to see the results.

Auditioning fabrics for a crazy patchwork garment

ℐhe Crazy Patchwork Method

Each garment begins with a muslin base. You may use a commercial pattern or one of the designs in this book, composed of a group of squares and rectangles. In either case, you will cut each piece from muslin, make any required fitting adjustments, then cover the muslin with crazy patchwork. The following method has proved fail-safe for me and my students.

1. Begin with Patch #1. Cut a piece of fabric into a patch with 5 sides—somewhat like a lopsided house. Cut it from a square of fabric that is approximately 4" x 4". The size of Patch #1 plays a role in determining the sizes of the remaining patches. If you cut the first piece too small, you will end up with many short seams to embroider. I like to use larger pieces because I can also cover them with embroidery if I wish, in addition to covering the seams with lovely stitches. If your fabric selections include one with heavier texture, choose it for Patch #1. It will be easier to handle in this position. Place this patch at the center of the muslin square or rectangle.

2. For Patch #2, choose a fabric that looks good next to Patch #1. Lay the fabric, right side down, on top of Patch #1, lining up the raw edges.

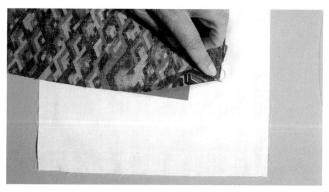

Note

I do not cut a piece for Patch #2 from the yardage unless I want a particular motif from the inner portion of the design. This is easy and keeps fabric waste to a minimum. I rarely use pins and suggest you try doing without them to save time, not to mention wear and tear on your sewing machine.

3. Set the machine for 12 stitches per inch, then stitch ¼" from the raw edges. Do not backstitch, so it is easy to remove a stitch or two if necessary.

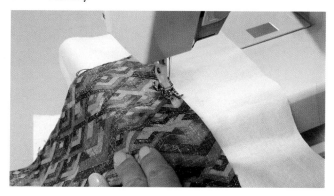

4. Flip the fabric for Patch #2 onto the muslin and press, making sure there are no pleats or tucks along the seam line.

5. Now cut the patch. Using the 2 straight edges of Patch #1 that are perpendicular to the seam you just stitched as a guide, make 2 cuts into the fabric. These cuts should be no longer than 6" to 8".

6. Make a third cut across the fabric at an angle. (Do not cut to a point.) Set the remaining fabric aside for additional patches.

7. Select a fabric for Patch #3. Place it face down along one of the new edges created with Patches #1 and #2 and line up the raw edges. Stitch ¼" from the raw edges, flip the fabric onto the muslin, and press.

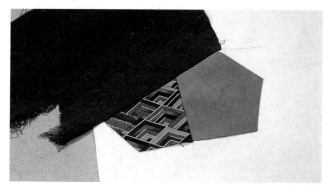

8. Cut Patch #3 in the same manner you cut Patch #2, extending the perpendicular edges with cuts into the fabric. Cut the end at an angle. As you make each cut, try to keep all sides no more than 6" to 8" long. This governs how you will cut the angled end.

9. Continue adding patches in the same manner to cover the muslin square or rectangle. Work either clockwise *or* counterclockwise around the center patch.

10. When the crazy patchwork reaches the outer edge of the muslin, make the 2 perpendicular cuts as usual, then flip the piece over and cut the fabric even with the muslin edge.

Note

If you follow the method described above, you won't have to sew any seams by hand. Remember to stitch, cut two straight lines, then cut the angled end. The patches will get larger as you reach the outer edges; cut the angles carefully so the seams don't get too long.

Patching with Special Fabrics

If you are using sheer or lace fabric, place it face down along the patchwork edge, then place an opaque fabric on top and align the raw edges of both layers with the patchwork edge. Use pins to hold the layers in place if necessary.

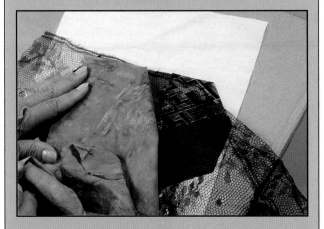

Synthetic suede fabric such as Ultra Suede does not ravel, so you do not have to use traditional seaming techniques. Instead, you may cut a straight edge, place it face up on top of the raw edge where you would normally stitch a patch, and use glue stick to hold it in place. Then cut the straight lines and the angle just as you would cut a fabric patch. This method avoids a very thick seam allowance. The glue holds the suede until embroidery stitches are added to hold it permanently in place.

Note

When using a commercial pattern, you will need to use some additional piecing techniques for the shoulder areas. See "Vest Pattern Selection and Patching" on pages 68–69.

Special Techniques for Crazy Patchwork

You can make an ordinary piece of fabric more interesting by using one of the following techniques to change its character and texture.

Scrunch and Press

Laces and sheer fabrics lend themselves best to this technique. Make sure your iron is preheated.

1. Dampen a piece of fabric that is larger than the patch you need, then scrunch it into a mass on the ironing board.

2. Press with the iron to create a variety of folds that provide excellent places to sew beads and charms. Adding these will hold the folds in place on the muslin foundation. You may also use embroidery stitches to anchor the folds; the fly stitch is one of my favorites for this method.

Note

If you use a sheer fabric for this technique, and it still looks sheer after scrunching, layer it over a piece of opaque fabric. Experiment with sheer fabrics. I have used one made of silk and metallic threads. It looks like organza and when you dampen it, it scrunches up on its own. If you press out the scrunching, it looks like cobwebs or gossamer angel wings. If I hadn't dared to dampen this fabric, I would not have discovered this unique texture.

Twist and Tuck

1. Cut narrow ribbon, cording, or braid into pieces longer than the crazy patch you wish to embellish.

2. Pin one end of the ribbon or cord outside one raw edge of a patch, then twist it across the patch and end it beyond the opposite raw edge. Pin in place. Do this with several pieces until the patch looks interesting, then hand stitch the ends in place or keep them pinned until you have added other patches to hold them in place.

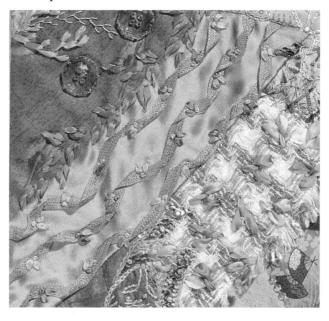

Note

Patches with twisted trims that you let dangle a bit are best used on the upper areas of a garment, where they won't be caught by fingers or jewelry. To use this technique lower on the garment, try tacking the twists with beads or decorative stitches.

If you wish to use wider ribbons, twist and tuck them, then press to create permanent folds. Tack in place with beads or embroidery stitches.

Fabric Fringe

Some fabrics, such as heavy slubbed silks and some loosely woven woolens, unravel before you can get them stitched in place. You can take advantage of this fringe and put it to decorative use. Using this method with heavier fabrics is a good way to eliminate a thick seam allowance, where these fabrics join others. (Thick seam allowances are more difficult to embroider and embellish.)

1. Pull and remove yarns along one edge of the fabric until you have created a fringe of the desired length. Pin the fringed edge of the fabric, right side up, along the straight edge where you would normally add the next patch. Make sure the fringe covers the raw edge of the previous patch. Machine or hand stitch in place just inside the fringe line. Cut 2 sides and angle as for the previous patches.

2. Embellish with embroidery, choosing a stitch to enhance the fringe, or add beads along the stitching line. Many times the machine stitching doesn't even show, so your options are numerous.

General Directions for All Garments

The garments in this book allow design freedom. Let your imagination guide you as you follow the directions for the vest or jacket of your choice. Because the garments are based on simple shapes, you have lots of flexibility regarding color and patchwork placement. For example, sometimes I prefer to make a vest or jacket back using a solid color or only one print. I cut that piece as I would the lining piece. If a panel is made of several small units, as with the back of the Scrappy Vest (page 60), you may add the size of the required units together and cut one piece instead. Don't forget to subtract the adjoining seam allowances.

All fabric yardage in this book is based on 42"-wide fabric. This allows for shrinkage and for using fabrics that are not the typical 44" width.

The Construction Process in a Nutshell

In general, you will follow these easy steps to make your garment.

1. Select the garment design you wish to make.

2. Select at least 12 different fabrics for the crazy patchwork.

3. Use muslin for the base pieces.

4. Make any necessary fitting adjustments. (See below.)

5. Cut the necessary muslin base pieces for the garment you are making. The directions for each garment include the correct measurements to cut each piece required for your size.

6. Cover each muslin base piece with crazy patchwork.

7. Add embroidery and other embellishments to each completed piece of crazy patchwork.

8. Assemble and finish the garment.

Fitting Adjustments

Yardage and cutting directions are given in three sizes for each of the roomy jacket and vest designs in this book: Small (6–8), Medium (10–12–14), and Large (16–18–20). All the garment designs in this book are oversize for a loose fit. Depending on how you like your garments to fit, you may be able to make your garment in a smaller size than you normally wear.

Because each design is based on simple shapes, size adjustments are easy to make. You can determine the finished shoulder, bustline, and hip measurements by adding up the width of the pieces required and subtracting ½" from the width of each piece.

For example, the finished hip measurement of the Scrappy Vest for the three sizes would be calculated by subtracting the ½" total seam allowance from the size of the required square, multiplying by 7, and adding the finished width of the two bands (4"). You can calculate the back length from neckline to finished bottom edge in a similar manner.

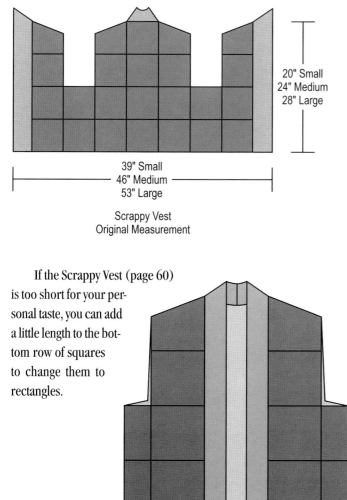

39" Small
46" Medium
53" Large

20" Small
24" Medium
28" Large

Scrappy Vest
Original Measurement

If the Scrappy Vest (page 60) is too short for your personal taste, you can add a little length to the bottom row of squares to change them to rectangles.

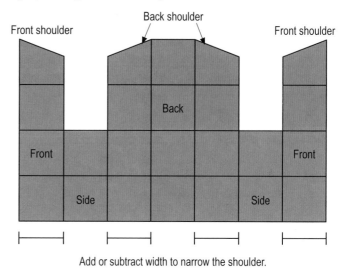

Make length adjustment to bottom row of units.

If you would like to adjust the shoulder width of a garment, add or subtract the required amount from the front and back pieces along the shoulder edge.

Front shoulder   Back shoulder   Front shoulder

Back

Front   Front

Side   Side

Add or subtract width to narrow the shoulder.

If the shoulder is the correct measurement but you need more room in the hip, and you're making one of the garments with side panels such as the Scrappy Vest, add equal amounts to the edges of the side panels and the bottom two rows of the front and back panels. Be aware that this adds the same amount of room in the underarm (top edge of upper side square).

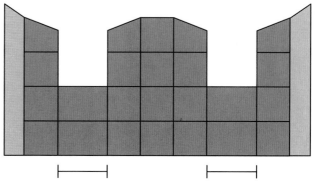

Widen the side panel squares to add hip width.

• *A few of the designs in the book have shaped shoulders or necklines. After cutting the muslin-base pieces according to the directions, lay them out and mark them to make sure you do the crazy patchwork on the correct side of the left and right pieces. (This is the suggestion of someone, namely me, who has one or two extra garment right fronts floating around her workroom.)*

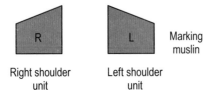

Right shoulder unit   Left shoulder unit   Marking muslin

• *You may add quilt batting to the garments for added warmth or styling. Use the yardage and cutting directions given for the lining pieces to cut the batting layer. The Himalayan Jacket (page 40) and the Safari Vest (page 54) are perfect for this purpose because there is only one shape each for the front, back, and sleeve. Layer the batting on top of the muslin for each piece, then do the patchwork on top of the batting, following the basic patchwork method.*

Finishing Techniques

The outer edges of the Tuxedo Vest (page 48), Safari Vest, and Himalayan Jacket are finished with binding. You can finish the edges of other garments in the same manner if you wish. Rather than make buttonholes in the actual patchwork, you can add button tabs.

Button Tabs

1. Measure the diameter of the button you wish to use, multiply the diameter by 2, then add ½". The total is the cut length for one tab. For example, if the button has a 1" diameter, you would cut the tab 2½" long (1" diameter x 2 + ½" = 2½" tab length).

2. Cut a 1¼"-wide strip of fabric long enough to make the required number of button tabs.

3. Fold the strip in half lengthwise, wrong sides together; press.

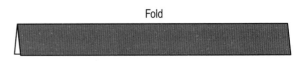

Fold

4. Open the pressed strip and fold the raw edges toward the crease so they meet at the center. Press.

Center fold

5. Fold in half again and press, enclosing the raw edges. Edgestitch through all layers, or slipstitch the two creased edges together. Cut the tab strip into the lengths determined in step 1.

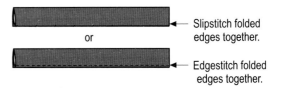

or

Slipstitch folded edges together.

Edgestitch folded edges together.

6. Fold and press the tabs as shown, and position at the garment edge where indicated in the directions. Pin or baste the tabs in place on the garment.

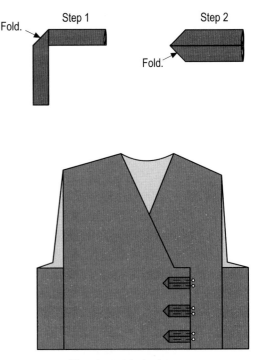

Fold.   Step 1   Step 2

Fold.

Pin or baste tabs in place.

Binding

Yardage is given for binding the Safari and Tuxedo Vests and the Himalayan Jacket. If you wish to bind the edges on any of the other designs, measure the edges you are going to bind and total those measurements to determine how much binding you will need. Add a few inches for seaming the strips together. Divide the total by 40" to give you the number of 1¼"-wide strips you will need to cut for the binding.

To bind the edges:

1. Cut the required number of 1¼"-wide strips, using rotary-cutting equipment. To join the strips, lay 2 ends right sides together and perpendicular to each other; draw a diagonal stitching line. Stitch, trim ⅛" from the stitching, then press the seam open.

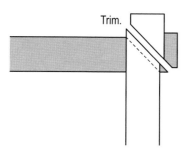

Trim.

2. Place the patchwork piece on top of the lining piece, wrong sides together, and pin or baste.

3. With right sides together, stitch the binding to the garment edge, ¼" from the raw edges.

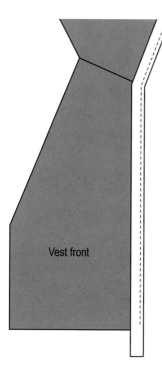

Vest front

4. Trim excess binding at the ends of each piece and press the binding toward the seam allowance, but do not turn it to the lining side yet.

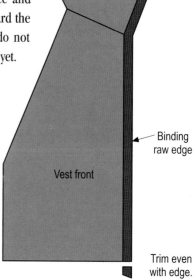

Binding raw edge

Vest front

Trim even with edge.

5. Sew the binding strip to the next edge, beginning at the end of the strip you just trimmed. Repeat until you have added a binding strip to all raw edges.

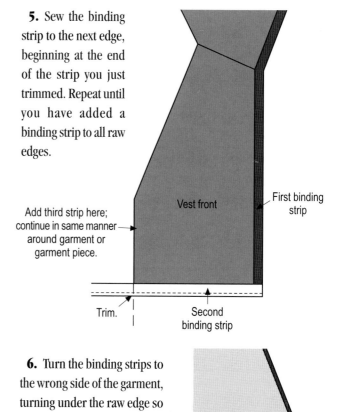

Add third strip here; continue in same manner around garment or garment piece.

Vest front

First binding strip

Trim.

Second binding strip

6. Turn the binding strips to the wrong side of the garment, turning under the raw edge so the fold just covers the stitching line. Slipstitch in place.

Slipstitch.

Crazy Rags Projects

Crazy Cache

This little bag is the perfect first project, especially if you have never done crazy patchwork. In addition, it can be crazy patched and embroidered all in one day. It's a great place to store jewelry or other treasures for traveling, and it makes a wonderful gift for someone special. In white lace and satin, it becomes a beautiful bridal keepsake.

French Beret

This classic beret with a contemporary flair takes only a little fabric—a great way to use favorite scraps. Patched in velvet or taffeta, it's the perfect fashion statement for the holidays. Synthetic suede is a nice option for the underside of the patched hat top.

Drawstring Handbag

Here's a fashionable and functional handbag for those who like a roomy tote. The crazy-patched lower portion provides the interest, and the fabric in the upper portion and binding acts as a frame for your work of art. Synthetic suede makes an excellent upper bag and base fabric. If you choose a lighter-weight fabric for these areas, strengthen it with a layer of fusible interfacing on the wrong side.

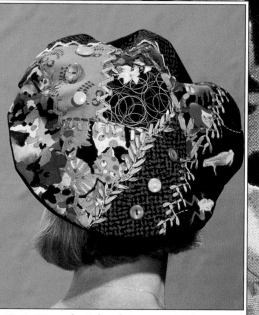

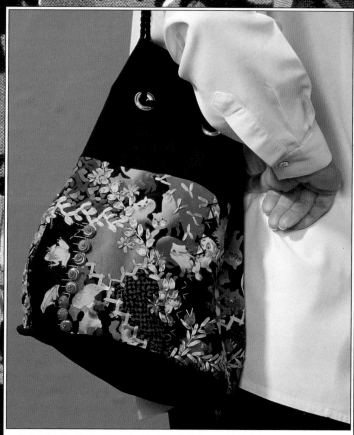

Cat's Meow by Deborah Brunner, 1995, Sarasota, Florida. Silk-ribbon embroidery and hand-dyed buttons add finishing touches to this bright beret made from favorite cat prints. It's a pur-r-r-fect partner for the Drawstring Handbag.

Cats Out of the Bag by Deborah Brunner, 1995, Sarasota, Florida. Like its companion beret, the drawstring handbag is embellished with silk-ribbon flowers and traditional embroidery stitches. Black Ultra Suede sets off the brightly colored print.

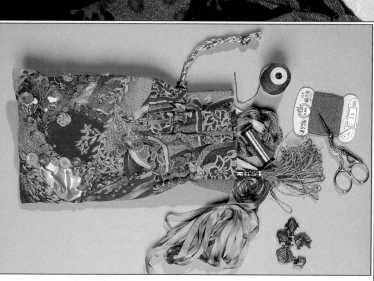

Goin' Crazy by Deborah Brunner, 1995, Sarasota, Florida. A bright orange-and-turquoise quilting cotton inspired this festive little bag, perfect for an evening out or for carrying a small assortment of sewing tools. Silk fabrics, silk-ribbon embroidery, and hand-dyed buttons add sparkle.

CRAZY CACHE

Materials

In addition to assorted fabric scraps totaling ⅛ to ¼ yard for the crazy patchwork, you will need the following materials:

Muslin • 6½" x 12½" rectangle	
Lining/border fabric • 12½" x 14" rectangle	
Drawstring • 1 yd. cording	

Crazy Cache Construction

Use ¼"-wide seam allowances throughout.

1. Cover the 6½" x 12½" piece of muslin with crazy patchwork as described in "The Crazy Patchwork Method" on pages 10–14. Begin with the five-sided patch in the center of the rectangle.

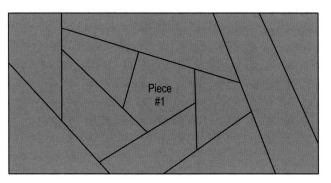

Crazy-patched rectangle

2. Embroider the seams as desired, referring to the "Crazy Cache Embroidery Pattern" on page 84.

3. Fold the crazy-patched piece in half crosswise, right sides together. Stitch ¼" from the short raw edges.

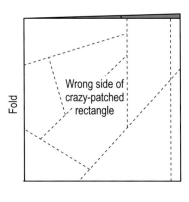

Fold

Wrong side of crazy-patched rectangle

4. Center the seam on one side of the tube and lightly press open. Stitch ¼" from the bottom edges through both layers.

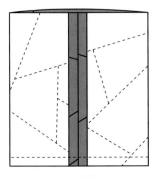

5. Turn bag right side out; lightly press along the bottom edge.

Lining Construction and Finishing

1. Fold the lining/border rectangle in half, right sides together, and stitch ¼" from the long edges, leaving a ½" opening 1½" from the top edge. Be sure to backstitch each time you start and stop. Center and press the seam as you did for the bag.

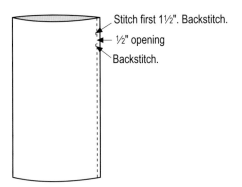

Stitch first 1½". Backstitch.
½" opening
Backstitch.

2. Slip the crazy-patched bag inside the lining, right sides together. Place the end of the lining with the ½"-long opening even with the top edge of the bag. Pin, then stitch ¼" from the raw edges. Turn under and press ¼" at the bottom edge of the lining.

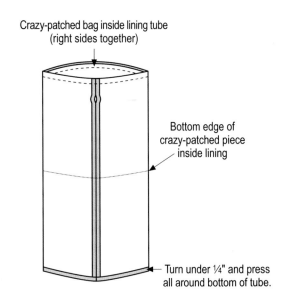

Crazy-patched bag inside lining tube
(right sides together)

Bottom edge of crazy-patched piece inside lining

Turn under ¼" and press all around bottom of tube.

3. To turn the bag right side out, pull the lining tube up and over the patchwork. Lightly press the seam toward the lining. Whipstitch the open ends of the lining together, or machine edgestitch.

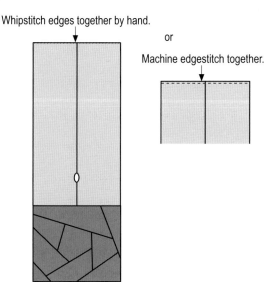

Whipstitch edges together by hand.

or

Machine edgestitch together.

4. Tuck the lining into the bottom of the crazy-patched bag and adjust so the lining forms a border at the top of the bag and lies flat and smooth inside the bag. Lightly press the top edge of the lining fabric. Stitch 1½" and 2" from the top edge of the bag to create a casing for the drawstring.

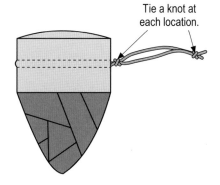

1½"   2"

5. Securely attach the drawstring cording to a safety pin and draw the cord through the casing twice. Adjust the drawstring ends so they are an even length. With the bag fully open, tie a knot at the opening, then tie one near the end as shown. Trim as needed.

Tie a knot at each location.

FRENCH BERET

Materials

In addition to assorted fabrics totaling ⅛ yard for the crazy patchwork, you will need the following materials:

Muslin • 13" x 13" piece	
Beret base • 13" x 13" piece	
Binding • 1 strip, 1¼" x 25", of fabric or grosgrain ribbon	
Lining • 13" x 26" piece	

Cutting

Using a compass, draw a 12½"-diameter circle on the wrong side of the muslin and the fabric for the beret base. Draw 2 circles on the lining fabric.

Note

Use a 12½"-diameter dinner plate as a template if you prefer.

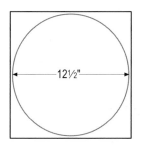

12½"

Beret Construction

Use ¼"-wide seam allowances throughout.

1. Cover the muslin circle with crazy patchwork. Begin with the five-sided patch in the center of the circle as described in "The Crazy Patchwork Method" on pages 10–14. Embroider as desired.

2. To shape the head opening in the beret base, use the following formula:

a. Measure the circumference of your head, using a tape measure as shown.

b. Divide your head circumference by 3.15 and round up or down to the nearest ¼", then subtract ½". This is the diameter of the circle for the head opening in the beret base and lining.

For example: $21.5 \div 3.15 = 6.82$

6.82 rounded to the nearest ¼" $= 6.75$

$6.75 - .50 = 6.25$ (6¼") head opening

3. Using the diameter determined in step 2b, draw a circle in the center of the beret base circle. Cut out the circle. Cutting for the beret base is now complete.

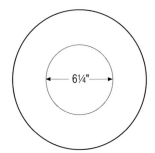

Cut circle out of beret base fabric.

Lining Construction and Finishing

1. Place the beret base on top of 1 of the lining circles and trace around the edge of the inner circle. Cut out the center circle for the lining ring.

2. Place the lining circle on top of the lining ring, *right sides together*. Place the crazy-patched circle on top of the lining circle, *wrong sides together*. Place the beret base on top of the patched circle, *right sides together*.

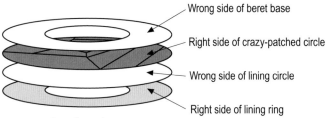

Wrong side of beret base

Right side of crazy-patched circle

Wrong side of lining circle

Right side of lining ring

Layering order

3. Pin the layers together with raw edges even. Stitch ¼" from the raw edges. Trim all layers *except the beret base* to ⅛".

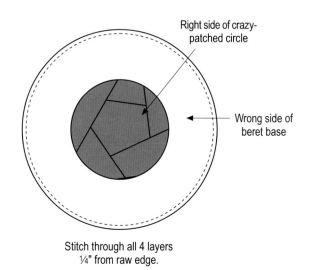

Right side of crazy-patched circle

Wrong side of beret base

Stitch through all 4 layers
¼" from raw edge.

4. Turn the beret base right side out through the center opening. Lightly press the seam along the outer edge. Pin or baste the raw edges of the opening together.

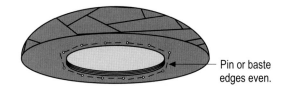

Pin or baste edges even.

5. Cut a binding strip 1¼" wide and the length of your head circumference (step 2a of "Beret Construction") + ½". You may substitute a similar length of 1"-wide grosgrain ribbon or a 1"-wide strip of synthetic suede.

6. Bind the raw edges of the opening as described in "Binding" on page 17.

Note

If you are binding the beret with synthetic suede or ribbon, do not turn under ¼" of the binding before sewing it in place. Turn the ribbon or suede to the inside, pin or baste the free edge in place, and machine stitch in-the-ditch from the right side of the beret.

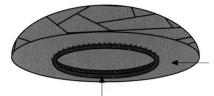

Right side of beret base

Binding with ribbon or suede strip

DRAWSTRING HANDBAG

Materials

In addition to assorted fabrics totaling ¼ to ⅜ yard for the crazy patchwork, you will need the following materials:

Muslin • ¼ yd.	
Upper bag, binding, and base • ⅜ yd.	
Lining • ½ yd.	
Interfacing • 1 yd. fusible (medium weight)*	
Drawstring • 3 yds. cording	
Grommets •12 purchased grommets, ⁷⁄₁₆" in diameter	

For fabrics other than synthetic suede

Cutting

Muslin • 4 squares, each 8½" x 8½"	
Upper bag fabric • 1 piece, 7" x 32"	
Base fabric • 10½"-diameter circle	
Lining • 1 piece, 15" x 32", 10½"-diameter circle	
Optional interfacing • 1 piece, 7" x 32", 10½"-diameter circle	

Handbag Construction

Use ¼"-wide seam allowances throughout.
Press seams open unless otherwise directed.

1. Cover the 4 muslin squares with crazy patchwork as described in "The Crazy Patchwork Method" on pages 10–14. Begin with the five-sided patch in the center of each square. Embroider as desired.

2. Arrange the pieces for the lower handbag as desired and sew together to create a tube. Press.

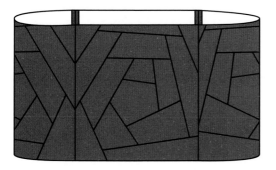

3. If you are using a fabric other than synthetic suede, fuse the interfacing to the wrong side of the upper handbag rectangle and the base circle.

4. With right sides together and raw edges even, fold the upper bag rectangle in half crosswise and stitch ¼" from the short end. Press seam open.

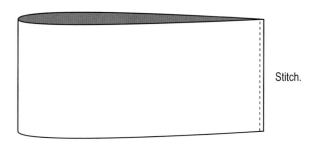

Stitch.

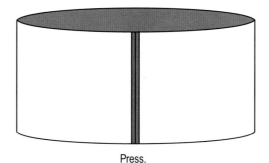

Press.

5. With right sides together, raw edges even, and the upper bag seam aligned with one of the seams in the lower bag section, stitch ¼" from the raw edges. Press the seam open and turn the bag right side out.

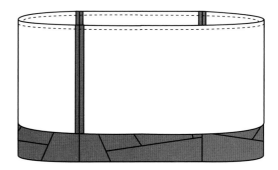

Lining Construction and Finishing

1. With right sides together, fold the lining rectangle in half crosswise and stitch ¼" from the short end. Press.

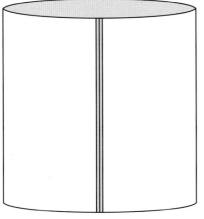

Stitch.

Press.

2. Pin the lining to the bag upper edge with right sides together, raw edges even, and the seams matching. Stitch ¼" from the raw edges.

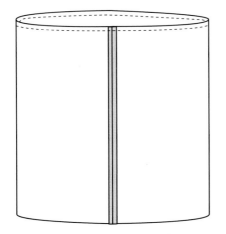

3. Turn the bag right side out and adjust the lining so both layers of the bag lie flat. Lightly press the upper finished edge and pin the bottom raw edges together. Baste.

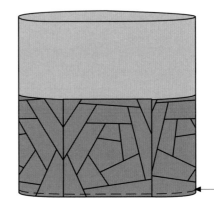

Baste bottom edge of lining and outer bag together.

4. Place the lining circle on top of the bag bottom circle, *wrong sides together.* Baste.

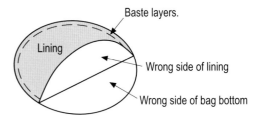

Baste layers.

Lining

Wrong side of lining

Wrong side of bag bottom

5. Pin the bottom circle to the bottom edge of the bag with the bottom lining and bag lining facing each other. (The seam will be on the outside of the finished bag.) Stitch ¼" from the raw edge.

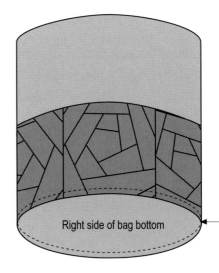

Right side of bag bottom

Sew bottom to bag body.

6. Cut a 1½" x 32" strip of binding and bind the raw edge of the bottom seam as shown on page 17.

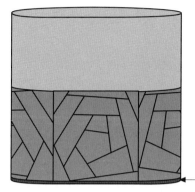

← Bind the bottom edge.

Note

If you are binding the handbag with synthetic suede, do not turn under ¼" on the remaining edge of the binding. Instead, turn it to the bottom of the bag, baste in place, then stitch in-the-ditch on the bag side and trim close to the stitching.

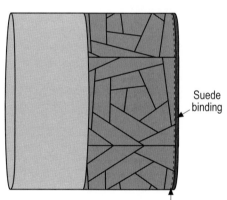

Suede binding →

Stitch in-the-ditch
from right side.

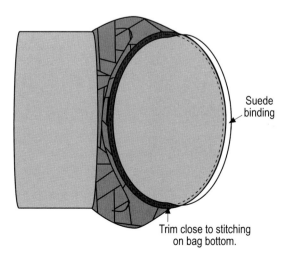

Suede binding →

Trim close to stitching
on bag bottom.

7. To mark the placement for 12 grommets, measure 2½" from the upper edge of the bag and make marks at approximately 2⅝" intervals. Use pins or a water-soluble marker. Double-check placement for accuracy before applying the grommets, following package directions.

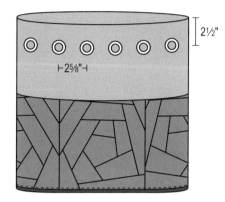

2½"

⊢ 2⅝" ⊣

8. Weave the cording through the grommets 2 times around, then adjust so the ends are even. Tie a knot and trim the ends.

Mandarin Coat

A stylized mandarin collar graces the off-center front closure of this roomy and exotic jacket. An innovative, button-back treatment adds wrist shaping to the full sleeves. Decorative machine embroidery in gold metallic thread embellishes the back and sleeves, while the front panels are heavily embellished with hand embroidery, beads, charms, and buttons. For a fabulous winter warmer, cut the patches from wool and embellish with more traditional embroidery stitches done in perle cotton.

Autumn Leaves *by Deborah Brunner, 1995, Sarasota, Florida. The front panels of this evening coat were hand embroidered with silk ribbon and embellished with antique glass buttons and beads. A combination of silk and cotton fabrics reflect the glorious colors of fall in Michigan. The patches on the sleeves and back of the Mandarin Coat are covered with machine-embroidered leaves in gold metallic thread. Antique glass buttons with a bronze metallic overlay grace the front closure and sleeves.*

Materials

In addition to assorted fabrics totaling approximately 2 to 3 yards for crazy patchwork, you will need the following materials:

	Small	Medium	Large
Muslin	1¼ yds.	1½ yds.	2¼ yds.
Collar, front, and sleeve bands	¾ yd.	⅞ yd.	⅞ yd.
Lining	1⅜ yds.	1⅝ yds.	2½ yds.
Interfacing	1½ yds.	1⅝ yds.	1¾ yds.
1"-diameter buttons	6	6	6

Optional: One pair of ⅜"- to ¾"-thick, raglan-style shoulder pads

Cutting

Fabric	Garment Section	No. of Pieces	Small	Medium	Large
Muslin	Fronts, back, and sleeves	6	12½" x 12½"	14" x 14"	15½" x 15½"
		6	9½" x 12½"	11" x 14"	12½" x 15½"
Lining	Right front	1	12½" x 24½"	14" x 27½"	15½" x 30½"
	Left front and sleeves	3	9½" x 24½"	11" x 27½"	12½" x 30½"
	Back	1	24½" x 24½"	27½" x 27½"	30½" x 30½"
Collar*		1	5½" x 25"	5½" x 27"	5½" x 27"
Interfacing*		1	5½" x 25"	5½" x 27"	5½" x 27"
Front band*		2	6½" x 24"	6 ½" x 27"	6½" x 30"
Interfacing*		2	6½" x 24"	6½" x 27"	6½" x 30"
Sleeve bands		2	6½" x 24½"	6½" x 27½"	6½" x 30½"
Interfacing**		2	6½" x 24½"	6½" x 27½"	6½" x 30½"

*The collar and front band pieces cut are a little long; you will trim them later.

**If you would like a softer sleeve edge, omit the interfacing in the sleeve band.

Coat Construction

Use ¼"-wide seam allowances throughout.

1. To shape the right front neckline, trim 1 of the muslin squares as shown for the size you are making. Label, using a pencil and marking very lightly.

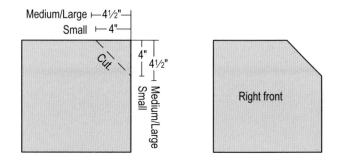

2. To shape the left front neckline, trim 1 of the muslin rectangles as shown for the size you are making. Label, using a pencil and marking very lightly.

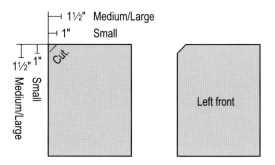

3. Cover the shaped muslin pieces and all remaining muslin pieces with crazy patchwork as described in "The Crazy Patchwork Method" on pages 10–14. Begin with the five-sided patch in the center of each piece.

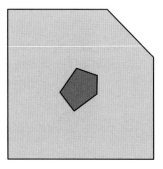

4. In addition to the shaped front pieces, select 1 crazy-patched square and 1 crazy-patched rectangle for the front. Embroider these 4 pieces as desired. Embellish the remaining squares and rectangles for the back and sleeves with simple embroidery, referring to Embroidery Tip #8 on page 72.

5. Arrange the pieces for each front as shown. Sew the pieces together and press the seams open.

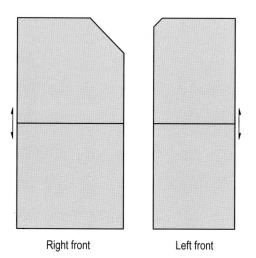

Right front   Left front

6. Arrange the remaining crazy-patched squares for the back as desired. Sew the pieces together and press the seams open.

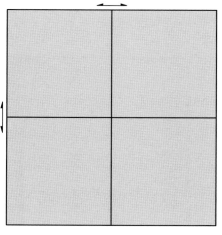

Back

7. Arrange the remaining rectangular pieces for the sleeves as desired. Sew the pieces together and press the seams open.

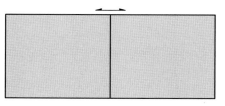

Sleeve

8. With right sides together, sew the front and back panels together at the shoulders. Press the seams open.

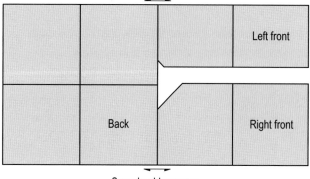

Sew shoulder seams.

9. With right sides together and the sleeve and shoulder seams matching, stitch the sleeves to the coat. Press the seams open.

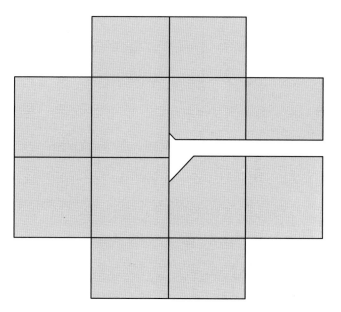

10. With right sides together, sew the side and sleeve seams, pivoting at the underarm corner. Clip to, but not through, the stitching as shown; press seams open. Turn the jacket right side out.

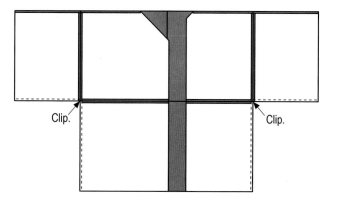

Clip.   Clip.

Lining Construction and Finishing

1. To add shoulder pads, pin them in place along the shoulder seam line, try on, and adjust as needed. Sew the pads in place along the seam line.

2. To shape the neckline on the right and left front lining panels, place them *wrong side up* and trim as shown.

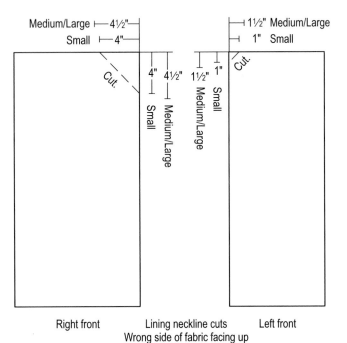

Right front Lining neckline cuts Left front
Wrong side of fabric facing up

3. Fold the sleeve lining rectangles in half crosswise and clip the fold ⅛" at one end to mark the center.

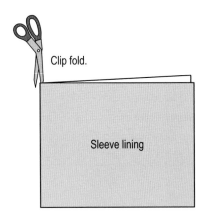

Clip fold.

Sleeve lining

4. With right sides together, sew the front and back lining panels together at the shoulders. Press the seams open. Sew the sleeves to the armhole edges, matching the snip on each sleeve to the corresponding shoulder seam. Press the seams open.

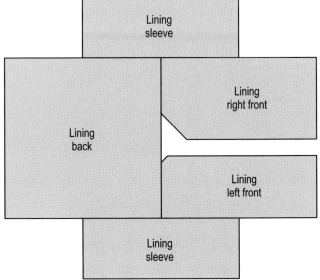

5. With right sides together, sew the side and sleeve seams as shown in step 10 of "Coat Construction" on page 29.

6. With right sides together and using a ¼"-wide seam allowance, stitch the lining to the coat at the bottom edge only.

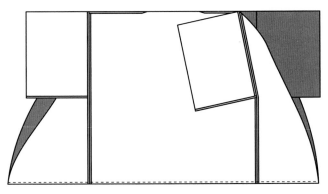

Sew lining to coat along bottom edge only.

7. Turn the lining to the inside and press the bottom edge carefully. Baste the raw edges of the coat and lining together except at the back neckline.

8. Measure 1" from the neckline edge at the center back and draw a shallow curve that tapers back to nothing at the shoulder seams. Cut on the drawn line.

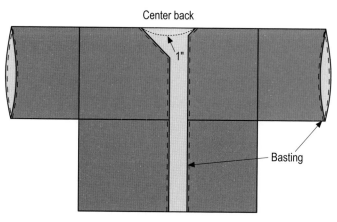

Shaping the back neckline

9. Sew or fuse the interfacing to the wrong side of the collar and the front and sleeve bands. Turn under and press ¼" along one long edge of the collar and each front band.

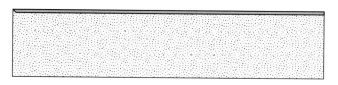

Turn under ¼" on one long edge of collar and front bands.

10. Pin 1 front band to the edge of the coat right front, right sides together, raw edges even, and the top edge of the band extending ¼" above the angled neckline edge. It will also extend below the bottom edge of the coat. Stitch ¼" from the raw edges.

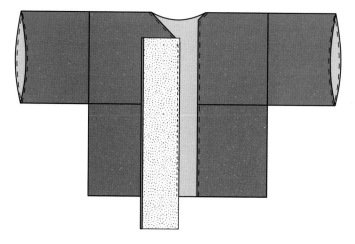

11. Turn the band to the inside, placing the folded edge along the band seam line, and press carefully. Turn the band back onto itself, right sides together; stitch across the bottom edge a scant ¹⁄₁₆" below the bottom edge of the coat. Trim ⅛" to ¼" from the stitching and clip the corner. Turn right side out.

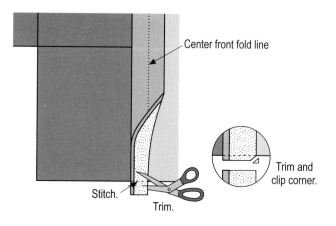

12. Repeat steps 10 and 11 for the left front band.

13. Turn the right and left front bands to the inside, placing the folded edge along the stitching lines; press carefully and slipstitch in place.

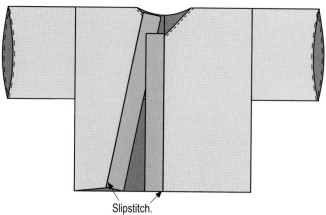

Slipstitch.

14. Trim the collar where it extends above the angled cut of the neckline, matching the neckline angle of each front.

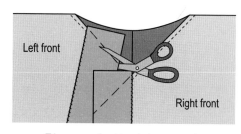

Trim excess front band at same angle
as neckline of each front.

15. With right sides together and raw edges even, pin the collar to the neckline edge. Begin pinning on the left side, extending the band ¼" beyond the folded edge of each front band. Stitch ¼" from the raw edges. Press the seam toward the collar.

16. Turn the collar to the inside, placing the folded edge along the stitching, and press carefully.

17. Turn the collar back onto itself, right sides together, and stitch across each end from the outer edge of the front band straight to the folded edge of each front band. Trim the excess band ⅛" to ¼" from the stitching, clip the corners, and turn right side out.

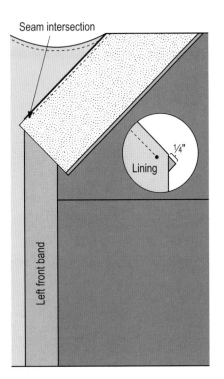

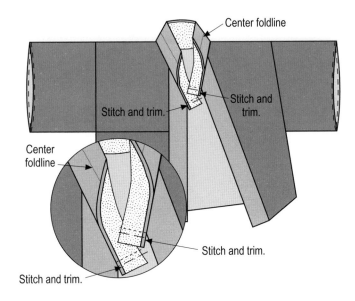

18. Fold each sleeve band in half crosswise, raw edges even. Stitch ¼" from the short end and press the seam open. Turn under and press ¼" along one long edge of each band.

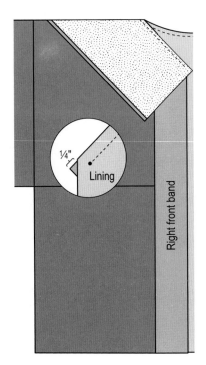

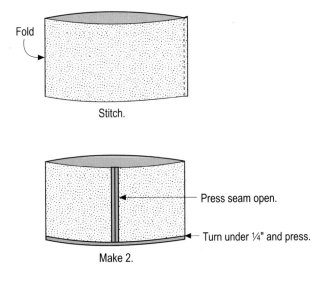

19. With right sides together, raw edges even, and underarm seams matching, stitch a sleeve band to each sleeve edge.

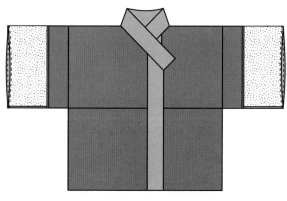

Stitch 1 sleeve band to each sleeve.

20. Turn the collar and sleeve bands to the inside, placing the folded edges along the stitching lines. Press carefully and slipstitch in place.

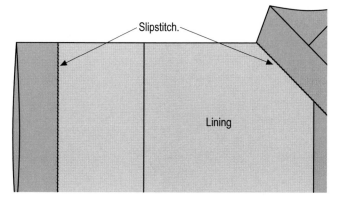

Slipstitch.

Lining

21. Following the directions on page 16, cut 6 button tabs from the remaining band fabric and construct the tabs. Make the tabs long enough to fit around the button comfortably and extend to the inner edge of the right front band. If you prefer, you may use purchased or handmade frog closures instead of button tabs.

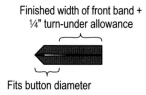

Finished width of front band +
¼" turn-under allowance

Fits button diameter

22. Turn under and press ¼" at each end of each tab. Position and slipstitch the tabs in place, placing the first tab just below the collar seam line as shown above right. Position the remaining

front tabs as desired. With front bands overlapped, mark button positions and sew buttons in place.

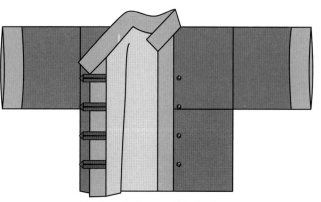

Hand sew buttons and tabs in place.

23. Position one of the remaining button tabs at the underarm seam at the bottom edge of each sleeve and slipstitch in place as shown for the front button tabs.

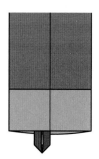

24. Turn each sleeve up so the tab meets the band seam line. Sew a button in place on the sleeve. If you prefer, you can make a deeper fold to adjust the bottom of the sleeve.

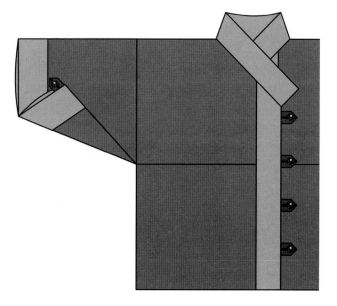

Kimono Jacket

Though slightly oversized, this jacket is similar to a traditional kimono. The addition of underarm gussets adds a contemporary flair and lots of ease for wearing comfort. The design is versatile: the fabrics you select will determine whether your jacket takes you out for an elegant evening or down home on the ranch for casual fun.

Orange and Purple Passion by Deborah Brunner, 1994, Williamston, Michigan. I love these colors! I used a combination of silk, rayon, and cotton fabrics to crazy patch the Kimono Jacket. Silk ribbon and a variety of threads were used to embellish the bright fabrics. Crystal facets from one of my grandmother's necklaces add a nostalgic touch. A special thank-you goes to Mesee for carrying the best selection of orange and purple silk fabrics!

Materials

In addition to assorted fabrics totaling approximately 2 to 2½ yards for the crazy patchwork, you will need the following materials:

	Small	Medium	Large
Muslin	1⅛ yds.	1½ yds.	1⅞ yds.
Lining	1¼ yds.	1⅝ yds.	1⅞ yds.
Sleeve bands and neckbands	⅝ yd.	⅞ yd.	1 yd.
Interfacing	⅝ yd.	⅞ yd.	1 yd.

Optional: One pair of shoulder pads, ½" to ¾" thick

Cutting

Fabric	Garment Section	No. of Pieces	Small	Medium	Large
Muslin	Back	8	10½" x 10½"	12½" x 12½"	14½" x 14½"
	Gussets	2	7½" x 7½"	8" x 8"	8½" x 8 ½"
	Fronts	4	7½" x 10½"	9½" x12½"	11½"x 14½"
	Sleeves	4	10½" x 10½"	12½" x 12½"	14½"x 14½"
Lining	Back	1	20½" x 20½"	24½" x 24½"	28½" x 28½"
	Gussets	2	7½" x 7½"	8" x 8"	8½" x 8½"
	Fronts	2	7½"x 20½"	9½" x 24½"	11½" x 28½"
	Sleeves	2	10½" x 20½"	12½" x 24½"	14½" x 28½"
Sleeve band		2	5½" x 20½"	5½" x 24½"	5½" x 28½"
Interfacing*		2	5½" x 20½"	5½" x 24½"	5½" x 28½"
Neckband**		2	5½" x 25½"	5½" x 29½"	5½" x 33½"
Interfacing**		2	5½" x 25½"	5½" x 29½"	5½" x 33½"

If you would like a softer sleeve edge, omit the interfacing in the sleeve band.

**The neckband and neckband interfacing pieces are cut a little long; you will trim them later.*

Jacket Construction

Use ¼"-wide seam allowances throughout.

1. To shape the underarm gussets, cut the 2 small muslin squares in half once diagonally.

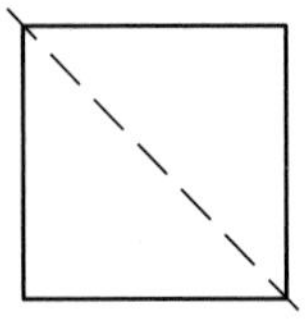

2. Cover all muslin squares and rectangles with crazy patchwork as described in "The Crazy Patchwork Method" on pages 10–14. Begin with the five-sided patch in the center of each piece.

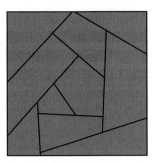

Crazy-patched square

3. Embroider the large rectangles for the front, adding as much embellishment as you wish. Embellish the squares for the jacket back and sleeves with simpler embroidery as described in Embroidery Tip #8 on page 72.

4. Arrange the 4 completed rectangles for the front as desired and sew together. Press the seams open.

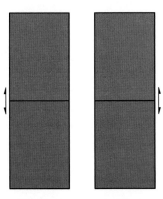

Right front   Left front

5. Arrange pieces for the back in the desired order and sew the pieces together. Press the seams open.

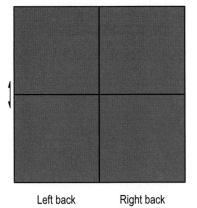

Left back   Right back

6. Arrange pieces for each sleeve in the desired order, adding the gussets at the outer edges as shown. Sew the pieces together and press all seams open.

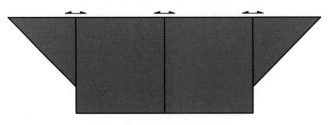

Sleeve and gussets

7. With right sides together, sew the front and back panels together at the shoulders. Press the seams open.

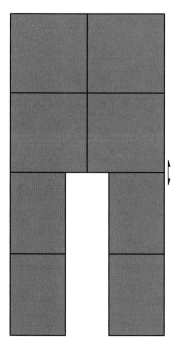

Sew shoulder seams.

8. With right sides together, sew the sleeve panels to the jacket, matching the center seam of each sleeve to the shoulder seam of the jacket. Press the seams open.

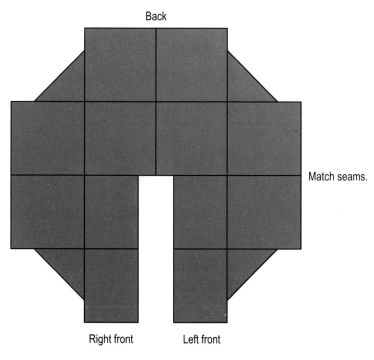

Back

Match seams.

Right front   Left front

9. With the right sides together, sew the side, gusset, and sleeve seams, pivoting at the gusset points. Clip to, but not through, the stitching at each end of the gusset. Press the seams open.

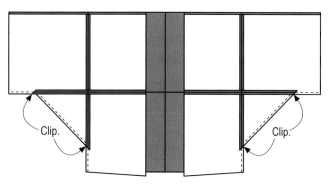

Clip.   Clip.

Lining Construction and Finishing

1. If you wish to add raglan-style shoulder pads to your jacket, pin them in place along the shoulder seams and try on the jacket. Adjust as needed and hand sew in place to the shoulder seam allowance.

2. With right sides together, sew the front and back lining panels together at the shoulders. Press the seams open.

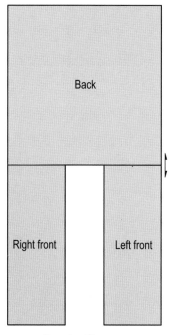

Back

Right front   Left front

Sew shoulder seams.

3. To shape the underarm gussets, cut the 2 small lining squares in half once diagonally as you did with the muslin gusset pieces in step 1 of "Jacket Construction" on page 36.

4. Sew the gussets to the sleeve panels; press the seams open.

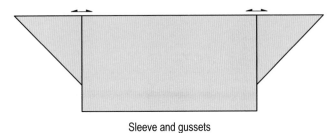

Sleeve and gussets

5. Fold each sleeve panel in half crosswise and make an ⅛"-long clip at one end of the fold to mark the center. With right sides together, sew the sleeve panels to the jacket lining, matching the center of each sleeve panel with the corresponding shoulder seam. Press the seams open.

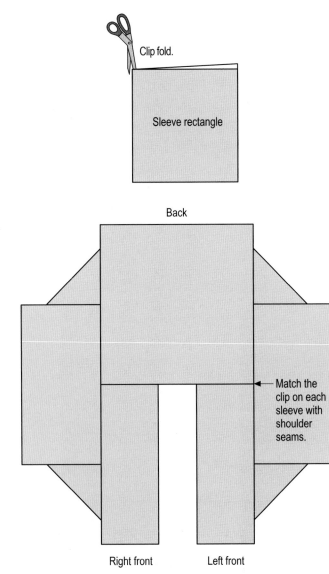

Clip fold.

Sleeve rectangle

Back

Match the clip on each sleeve with shoulder seams.

Right front   Left front

6. With right sides together, stitch the side, gusset, and sleeve seams as shown in step 9 of "Jacket Construction." Clip to, but not through, the stitching at each end of the gusset. Press the seams open.

7. With right sides together and using a ¼"-wide seam allowance, stitch the lining to the jacket along the bottom edge only.

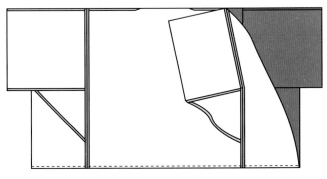

Sew lining to coat along bottom edge only.

8. Turn the lining to the inside of the jacket, wrong sides together, and press the bottom edge carefully. Baste the raw edges of the jacket and lining together, except across the back neckline.

9. Measure 1" from the neckline edge at the center back and draw a shallow curve that tapers back to nothing at the shoulder seams. Cut on the drawn line.

Center back

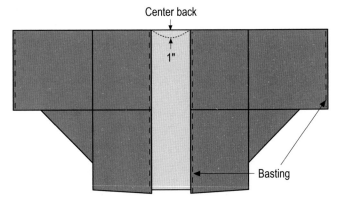

1"

Basting

10. Sew or fuse the interfacing to the wrong side of the sleeve band and neckband pieces.

11. With right sides together, stitch the 2 neckband pieces together at the center back as shown and press the seam open. Turn under and press ¼" along one long edge of the neckband.

Press.

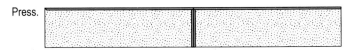

12. Fold each sleeve band in half crosswise and stitch ¼" from the raw edges. Press the seam open. Turn under and press ¼" along one edge of each sleeve band.

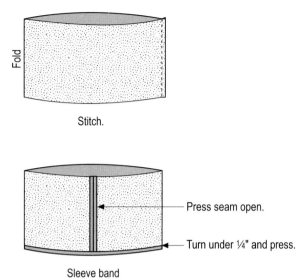

Stitch.

Press seam open.

Turn under ¼" and press.

Sleeve band

13. With right sides together and raw edges even, pin the neckband to the jacket neckline, placing the seam at the center back. Stitch ¼" from the raw edges. Note that the neckband should extend the same amount beyond each front bottom edge.

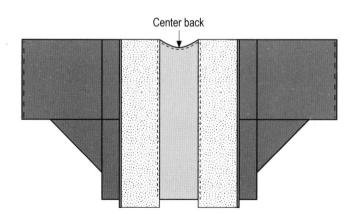

Center back

14. Turn the band to the inside, placing the folded edge along the stitching, and press carefully. Turn the band back onto itself, right sides together, and stitch across the bottom edges a scant ¹⁄₁₆" below the bottom edge of the jacket. Trim ⅛" to ¼" from the stitching and clip the corner to reduce bulk. Turn the band right side out and press.

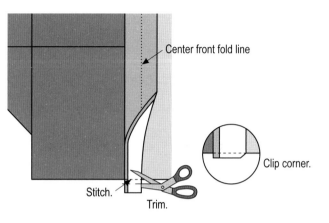

Center front fold line

Clip corner.

Stitch.

Trim.

15. With right sides together and raw edges even, pin each sleeve band to a sleeve bottom edge. Align the sleeve band seam with the sleeve seam. Stitch ¼" from the raw edges.

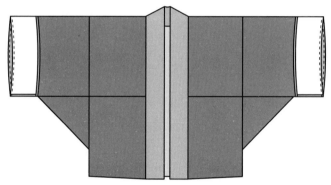

16. Turn the neck and sleeve bands to the inside, placing the folded edges along the stitching; press carefully. Slipstitch in place.

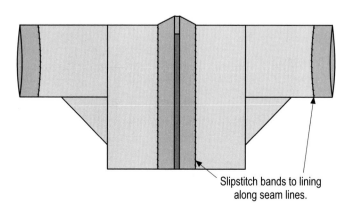

Slipstitch bands to lining along seam lines.

Himalayan Jacket

This jacket features a surplice front and collar. Buttons along the jacket armhole and button tabs along the shoulder edges of the sleeves make it possible to remove the sleeves, creating a vest—two garments for the time it takes to make one! Choose contrasting buttons to create focal points at the armholes if you wish. Of course, you can eliminate the sleeves and buttons if you want only a vest, since binding finishes the jacket edges. In a contrasting color, the binding looks like piping and draws attention to the structural lines of the jacket. In a matching color, it all but disappears.

Adventurina *by Deborah Brunner, 1995, Sarasota, Florida. Coral and taupe silk and cotton combine for this vest-only version of the Himalayan Jacket. The embroidery, a combination of silk ribbon and thread, is my contemporary expression of traditional embroidery stitches. All the glass buttons came from the collection of my husband's Grammie Brunner.*

Ode to Chi-Chi Moon Pie by *Deborah Brunner, 1995, Sarasota, Florida. I named this jacket for my Himalayan cat, who coveted the group of black and cream fabrics for her nap place. This jacket is an exercise in simplicity, from the use of only two-toned fabrics to the feather-stitch embroidery on all the patches. Buttons made from Alaskan caribou horn fit beautifully in the simple color scheme.*

Nouveau Favrile by *Maureen Carlson, 1995, Moline, Illinois. The title comes from the word* nouveau, *meaning new, and* Favrile, *a trade name registered in 1894 that applied to everything made by the House of Tiffany except jewelry. The name, derived from "fabricate," indicated that the object was handmade. This version of the Himalayan Jacket features an assortment of silk fabrics with rayon ribbon floss and hand-dyed silk-ribbon embroidery. The collar, back, and sleeves were cut from a hand-dyed silk, then heavily stipple quilted with gold metallic thread. The pieces were washed to shrink them for added texture. A collection of antique glass buttons finishes this exquisite piece.*

For added warmth, layer thin quilt batting on top of the muslin before doing the crazy patchwork. Do crazy patchwork on the sleeves and back as shown in the directions below, or cut the back and sleeves from a single fabric. If you prefer this option, see page 47 for the required yardage and cutting. There you will also find a yardage chart and cutting for the Himalayan Vest only. If you choose plain sleeves and back, consider embellishing them with machine quilting. Try a stippled pattern for allover texture, or try a grid or straight-line pattern for a more traditional look.

Materials

In addition to assorted fabrics totaling approximately 2½ to 3 yards for the crazy patchwork, you will need the following materials:

	Small	Medium	Large
Muslin	1⅞ yds.	2⅜ yds.	2¾ yds.
Lining	1⅞ yds.	2⅜ yds.	2¾ yds.
Neckband	⅛ yd.	⅛ yd.	⅛ yd.
Binding and tabs	½ yd.	½ yd.	⅝ yd.
Interfacing	¼ yd.	¼ yd.	¼ yd.
¾"-diameter buttons	28	30	30
1" to 1¼"-diameter buttons	3	4	4
Snaps	2	2	2

Optional: One pair of ⅜"- to ½"-thick shoulder pads.

Cutting

Be sure to cut the front, back, sleeve, and side pieces from the muslin and the lining fabric.

Fabric	Garment Section	No. of Pieces	Small	Medium	Large
Muslin and lining	Fronts and back	3	16" x 22"	18" x 24"	20" x 26"
	Sleeves	2	21" x 25"	22" x 29"	23" x 29"
	Side	2	4" x 8"	6" x 8"	8" x 10"
Neckband	Right band	1	4½" x 19"	4½" x 21"	4½" x 22"
Interfacing	Right band	1	4½" x 19"	4½" x 21"	4½" x 22"
Neckband	Left band	1	4½" x 14"	4½" x 14"	4½" x 14"
Interfacing	Left band	1	4½" x 14"	4½" x 14"	4½" x 14"

Jacket Construction

Use ¼"-wide seam allowances throughout.

1. To shape the shoulders and the front neckline edge, trim 2 of the muslin rectangles as shown for the size you are making.

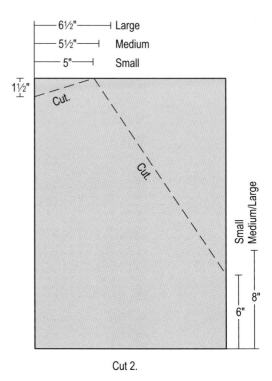

Cut 2.

2. Arrange the shaped pieces and label them as shown, using a pencil and marking very lightly.

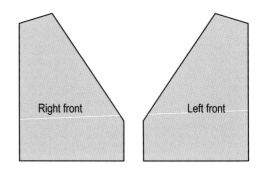

Right front   Left front

3. Use the remaining muslin rectangle for the vest back. Fold the rectangle in half lengthwise, raw edges even, and cut the shoulder angle as shown through both layers.

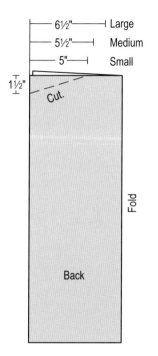

4. Cut the muslin sleeve pieces as shown for the size you are making.

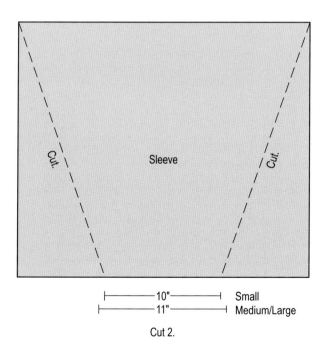

5. Cover the muslin right front, sleeves, and back pieces with crazy patchwork as described in "The Crazy Patchwork Method" on pages 10–14. Begin with the five-sided patch in the center of each piece's widest section.

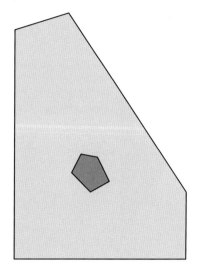

6. Since only a portion of the left front will be visible when you wear this jacket, you do not have to cover the entire piece with crazy patchwork. Place the right front on top of the left front, bottom and side edges even. Using a pencil, draw a light line on the left front along the right front neckline. Remove the muslin right front.

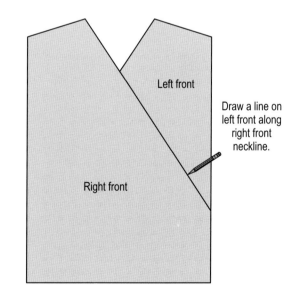

7. Do crazy patchwork on the left front, covering the section above the marked line and extending it ½" below the line. Cover the remainder of the left front with a single fabric, using the same stitch-and-flip method you used for the crazy patchwork. Trim even with the edges of the muslin and machine baste ¼" from the raw edges. (Crazy patching is not shown in the illustrations after this step.)

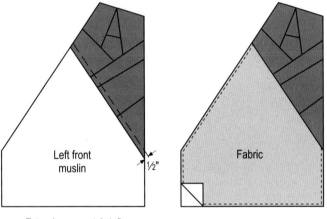

Extend crazy patch ½"
beyond marked line.

8. Embroider the fronts as desired and do simpler embroidery on the jacket back and sleeves as discussed in Embroidery Tip #8 on page 72.

9. With right sides together, sew the fronts and back together at the shoulders. Press the seams open.

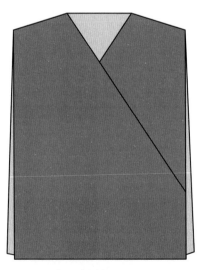

Sew shoulder seams.

10. If you wish to add shoulder pads to your jacket, pin them in place along the shoulder seam and try on the jacket. Adjust as needed and hand sew in place to the shoulder seam allowance.

Lining Construction and Finishing

1. Layer the lining front pieces, wrong sides together, and cut the shoulder angle and neckline as shown in step 1 of "Jacket Construction" on pages 42. Fold the back lining, wrong sides together and raw edges even, and cut the shoulder angle as shown in step 3 on page 43.

2. Sew the lining front and back together at the shoulders. Press the seams open.

3. Place the lining inside the jacket, wrong sides together. Baste ¼" from all raw edges except along the back neckline.

4. Measure 1" from the neckline edge at the center back and draw a shallow curve that tapers back to nothing at the shoulder seam. Cut on the drawn line.

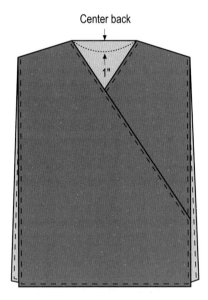

Center back

1"

5. Layer each sleeve with a sleeve lining, wrong sides together, and baste ¼" from the raw edges. Do the same with the side panels and corresponding lining pieces.

Note

If you elect not to crazy patch the sleeves and/or the side panels, layer a corresponding piece of muslin between the wrong sides of the outer and lining fabrics to add weight to the finished pieces. This will help them hang properly in relationship to the heavier front pieces.

6. Make 28 small button tabs for the small-size or 30 for the medium- or large-size jacket. Make these tabs to fit the ¾" buttons you will use along the sleeve edges. Make tabs to fit the 1" to 1¼" buttons for the front edge closure. Follow the directions for "Button Tabs" on page 16. Position the first tab at the center of the sleeve-head edge, then space the rest of the tabs 2" apart along the remaining edge. Pin or baste in place.

Sleeve center

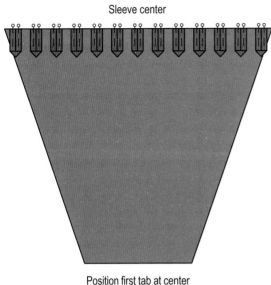

Position first tab at center
of sleeve-head edge.

7. Pin or baste button tabs on the right front edge, beginning ½" below the point where the neckline angle meets the straight edge and spacing them 2" apart.

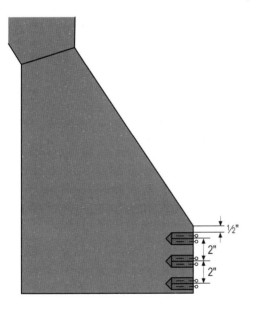

8. Sew or fuse the interfacing to the wrong side of the neckband pieces. With right sides together, stitch the 2 neckband pieces together at the center back and press the seam open.

Right neck band   Left neck band

9. With wrong sides together, fold the neckband in half lengthwise and press lightly. Turn the neckband right sides together and stitch ¼" from the raw edges at each short end. Clip corners. Turn right side out and press both ends.

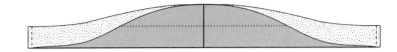

10. Referring to "Binding" on page 17, cut enough binding strips to finish all raw edges of the jacket body, sleeves, side panels, and neckband. Join strips as required, then bind the raw edges of each piece as shown.

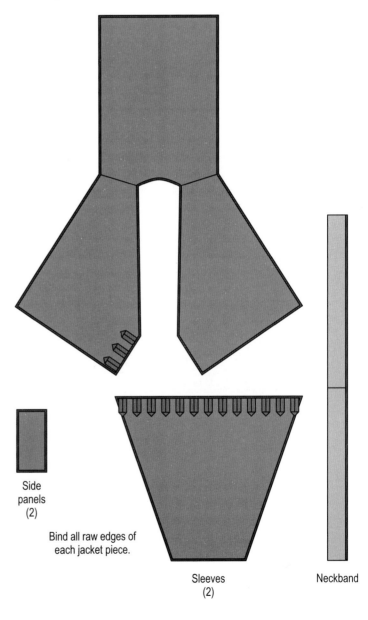

Side panels
(2)

Bind all raw edges of
each jacket piece.

Sleeves
(2)

Neckband

11. Press the button tabs out, over the binding at the right front edge and along each sleeve edge.

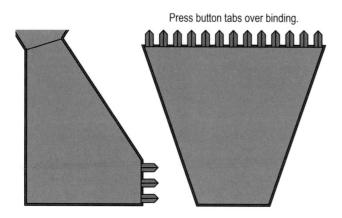

Press button tabs over binding.

12. Tuck the bound edges of each side panel under the bound edges of the side back and side front, with the inner edges of the binding aligned. Baste in place, then stitch in-the-ditch along the binding on the right side of the vest.

Back

Side panel

Front

Align inner edges of binding.

Stitch in-the-ditch.

13. Tuck the bound edge of the neckband under the bound edge of the jacket front, matching the center back seams of the neckband and the neckline and aligning the inner edges of the neckband and jacket bindings. Baste. The shorter half of the band should be on the left front. Stitch in-the-ditch along the inside edge of the neckline binding.

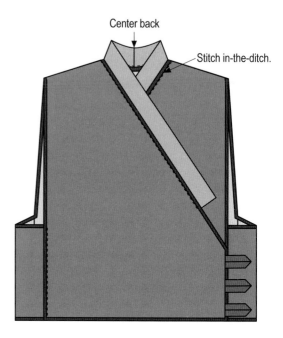

Center back

Stitch in-the-ditch.

14. Sew the buttons to the body of the jacket opposite the sleeve and front button tabs.

15. Sew the 2 snaps inside the jacket where the left front and right side panels meet, spacing them approximately 2" apart.

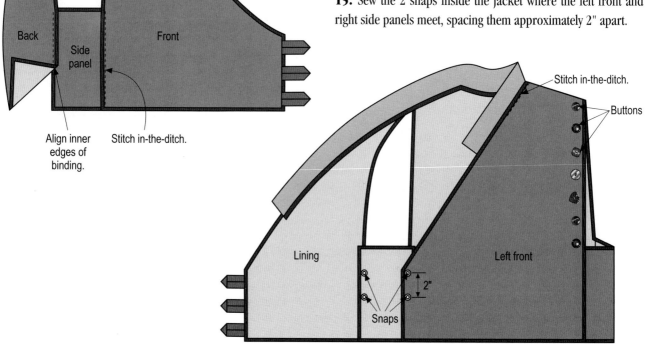

Stitch in-the-ditch.

Buttons

Lining

Left front

2"

Snaps

Add inner-edge snap closures.

16. Fold each sleeve, wrong sides together, with the inner edges of the underarm bindings aligned. Baste, beginning 4" from the underarm and ending 2" from the bottom edge. Stitch in-the-ditch where you have basted.

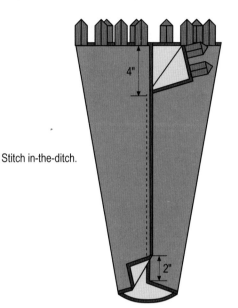

Stitch in-the-ditch.

Note

This is easier to do on a free-arm sewing machine. If you are having difficulty stitching by machine, you can do a short backstitch by hand along the inner edge of the binding.

17. Turn up the bottom edge of each sleeve to form a cuff if you wish.

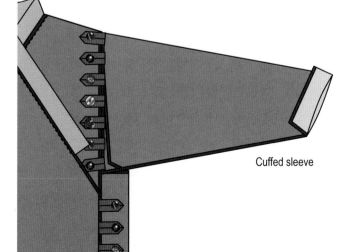

Cuffed sleeve

JACKET WITH PLAIN SLEEVES AND BACK

If you want to make a jacket with plain sleeves and back, the only change is you must add yardage for the sleeve and back fabric. All other materials and cutting remain the same. See the chart on page 42.

Materials

	Small	Medium	Large
Sleeves and back	1¼ yds.	2 yds.	2 yds.

VEST ONLY

Materials

In addition to assorted fabrics totaling approximately 1¾ to 2¼ yards for the crazy patchwork, you will need the following materials:

	Small	Medium	Large
Muslin	1¼ yds.	1⅜ yds.	1½ yds.
Lining	1¼ yds.	1⅜ yds.	1½ yds.
Neckband	⅛ yd.	⅛ yd.	⅛ yd.
Binding and tabs	¼ yd.	¼ yd.	⅜ yd.
Interfacing	¼ yd.	¼ yd.	¼ yd.
1"- to 1¼"-diameter buttons	3	4	4

Cutting

Be sure to cut the front, back, and side pieces from the muslin and the lining fabric.

Fabric	Garment Section	No. of Pieces	Small	Medium	Large
Muslin and lining	Fronts	2	16" x 22"	18" x 24"	20" x 26"
	Back	1	16" x 22"	18" x 24"	20" x 26"
	Sides	2	4" x 8"	6" x 8"	8" x 10"
Neckband	Right band	1	4½" x 19"	4½" x 21"	4½" x 22"
	Left band	1	4½" x 14"	4½" x 14"	4½" x 14"
Interfacing	Right band	1	4½" x 19"	4½" x 21"	4½" x 22"
	Left band	1	4½" x 14"	4½" x 14"	4½" x 14"

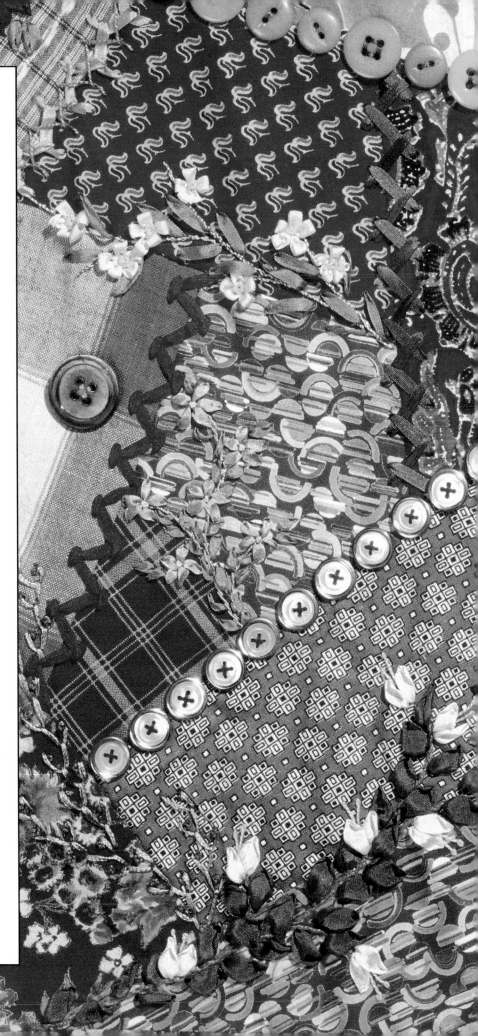

Tuxedo Vest

The lapels on this vest are created with a simple fold in each front. The side panels are triangles that attach to a back panel. Cover the back and sides with crazy patchwork, or cut the vest back and sides from a single fabric if you prefer. This is a very simple pattern, allowing lots of design freedom. It's the perfect complement to denim skirts and pants when done in everyday fabrics. Use dressier fabrics, and it becomes a sophisticated topper for a night on the town. In silk and lace, it is simply elegant.

Symphony by Deborah Brunner, 1995, Sarasota, Florida. I created this just to see the Tuxedo Vest in more sophisticated fabrics. I washed several pieces of silk douppioni to make them softer and more drapable. Hand-dyed silk-ribbon floral embroidery provides the perfect complement on the crazy-patched fronts.

Bell-Bottom Blues by Deborah Brunner, 1995, Sarasota, Florida. The discovery of the vintage red/blue/gold Italian cotton used on the lapels and gussets in this vest prompted me to reconsider wearing blue! Thanks to my friend Rhonda, I had three more vintage blue prints to add to the picture I painted with my fabric assortment. I used lots of my old buttons on this Tuxedo Vest.

Materials

In addition to assorted fabrics totaling approximately 1½ to 1¾ yards for the crazy patchwork, you will need the following materials:

	Small	Medium	Large
Muslin	⅝ yd.	1⅛ yds.	1¼ yds.
Lining fabric*	⅝ yd.	1⅛ yds.	1¼ yds.
Back and sides	½ yd	⅝ yd.	⅝ yd.
Binding	¼ yd.	¼ yd.	⅜ yd.

The front lining fabric will show on the lapels, so choose a fabric that works with the other fabrics in the crazy patchwork.

Cutting

Fabric	No. of Pieces	Small	Medium	Large
Muslin	3	14" x 18"	16" x 20"	18" x 22"
Lining	3	14" x 18"	16" x 20"	18" x 22"

Vest Construction

Use ¼"-wide seam allowances throughout.

1. To shape the shoulders and lapels, trim 2 of the muslin rectangles as shown, using rotary-cutting tools for straight, accurate cuts. *Set the cutaways aside for the side triangles.*

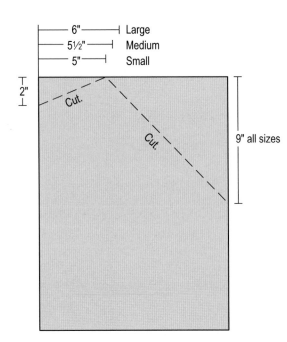

2. Arrange the shaped pieces and label them as shown, using a pencil and marking very lightly.

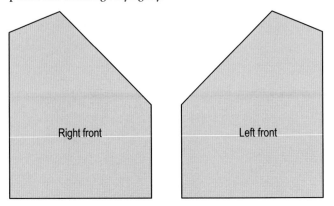

3. Cut the side triangles from the cutaways as shown.

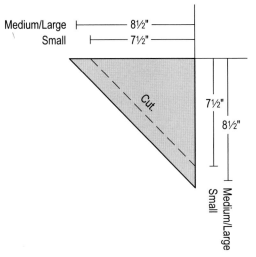

4. Fold the remaining rectangle for the back in half lengthwise, raw edges even. Cut the shoulder angle as shown.

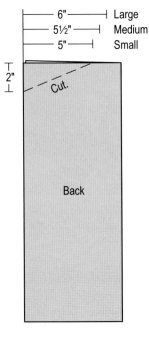

5. To form the lapels, mark 3" from the bottom edge of each vest front as shown. Fold the fabric back from the 3" mark to the intersection of the neckline and shoulder angles. Press.

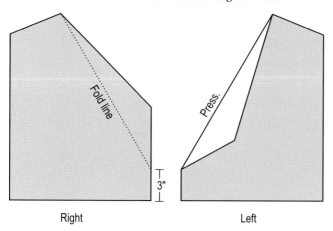

Right   Left

6. Cover the muslin pieces with crazy patchwork as described in "The Crazy Patchwork Method" on pages 10–14. Begin with the five-sided patch in the widest section of the vest front. Extend the crazy patchwork *only ¼" beyond the lapel fold line*. Cover the lapel with a single fabric. This creates a soft fold line for the finished lapel. (Crazy patching is not shown in the illustrations after this step.)

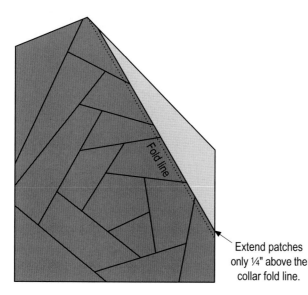

Extend patches
only ¼" above the
collar fold line.

7. Begin crazy patching the back of the vest by placing the five-sided patch in the center of the rectangle. Embroider all patchwork as desired. See "Hand Embroidery Stitch Guide" on pages 73–80.

Creative Option: Cut the vest back from a single fabric if you wish, following the cutting directions for the muslin and lining back pieces. Baste the vest back to the muslin back. You need the added weight of the muslin to balance the back with the heavier, crazy-patched front. Cut the triangular side pieces from a solid piece of fabric and back them with muslin too.

8. With right sides together, sew the front and back pieces together at the shoulders. Press the seams open.

Lining Construction and Finishing

1. Shape the shoulders and lapels and cut the triangles from the front lining pieces as shown in steps 1 and 3 of "Vest Construction" on page 50. Fold the back piece, wrong sides together with raw edges even. Cut the shoulder angles on the back piece as directed in step 4 on page 50.

2. Sew the front lining pieces to the back lining at the shoulders. Press the seams open.

3. Layer the vest and lining, *wrong sides together.* Baste together ¼" from the raw edges as shown.

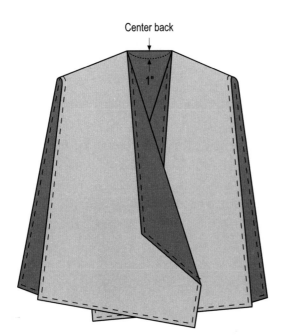

Baste ¼" from raw edges.

4. Measure 1" from the neckline edge at the center back and draw a shallow curve that tapers back to nothing at the shoulder seams. Cut on the drawn line.

Center back

1"

5. Place each muslin side triangle between the wrong sides of the vest and lining triangles. Baste together ¼" from the raw edges.

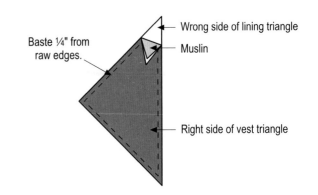

Baste ¼" from raw edges.

Wrong side of lining triangle

Muslin

Right side of vest triangle

6. Cut the binding strips 1¼" wide and bind all raw edges of the vest fronts, backs, and triangles as directed in "Binding" on page 17.

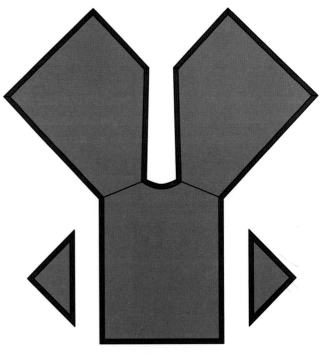

Bind all raw edges.

7. Position the long bound edge of each triangle under a side front edge as shown, so the inner edges of the binding are aligned. Stitch in-the-ditch along the inner edge of the binding on the side front edge.

8. Place the point of each side triangle on top of the corresponding side back edge as shown, overlapping about 2"; pin in place. Stitch in-the-ditch along the inner edge of the binding.

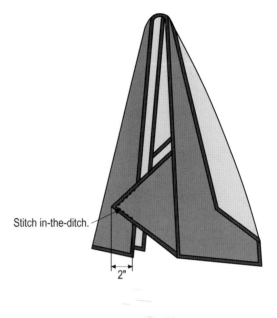

Stitch in-the-ditch.

2"

Stitch in-the-ditch.

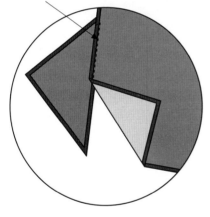

Stitch in-the-ditch.

Note

You may make a minor sizing adjustment at the side. Before stitching, pin the triangle in place on the back and try the vest on. Move the triangle point in or out for a closer or looser fit as desired. Stitch in-the-ditch. Add a decorative button or charm to the side triangle.

Creative Option: If you wish, you can make a buttonhole at the triangle point and sew a button to the vest back. Then button the triangle instead of stitching it in place.

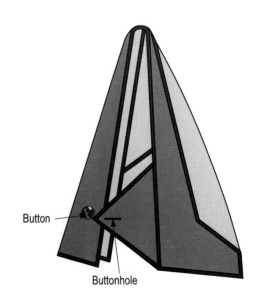

Button

Buttonhole

Safari Vest

An African-print fabric inspired the name of this easy vest. Individual side panels connect the front and back panels. A V-neckline with a simple collar completes the design. If you wish, layer with a thin quilt batting for additional warmth before adding the crazy patches. The back and side panels of this vest were cut from one fabric, but these panels can also be crazy patched if you prefer.

Out of Africa *by Deborah Brunner, 1994, Williamston, Michigan. It was a great year for African-inspired fabrics! The embroidery and embellishments reflect my impression of these wonderful designs. The funky women on the right front are my favorite embellishments, made with cowry shell buttons and Brazilian-rayon embroidery thread.*

Materials

In addition to assorted fabrics totaling approximately 1½ to 1¾ yards for the crazy patchwork, you will need the following materials:

	Small	Medium	Large
Muslin	⅝ yd.	1 yd.	1 yd.
Lining	⅝ yd.	1 yd.	1 yd.
Back and sides	⅝ yd.	¾ yd.	¾ yd.
Neckband	¼ yd.	¼ yd.	⅜ yd.
Binding	⅛ yd.	¼ yd.	¼ yd.
Interfacing	⅜ yd.	⅜ yd.	⅜ yd.
1¼"- to 1½"-diameter buttons	3	3	3

Cutting

Be sure to cut the front, back, and side pieces from the muslin and the lining fabric.

Fabric	Garment Section	No. of Pieces	Small	Medium	Large
Muslin and lining	Right front	1	11" x 21"	12" x 23"	13" x 24"
	Left front	1	9" x 21"	10" x 23"	11" x 24"
	Back	1	15" x 21"	17" x 23"	18" x 24"
	Sides	2	4" x 8"	6" x 10"	7" x 11"
Back and sides		1	15" x 21"	17" x 23"	18" x 24"
		2	4" x 8"	6" x 10"	7" x 12"
Neckband*		4	5" x 19"	5" x 20"	5" x 22"
Interfacing*		4	5" x 19"	5" x 20"	5" x 22"

The neckband and interfacing pieces are cut a little long; you will trim them later.

Vest Construction

Use ¼"-wide seam allowances throughout.

1. To shape the shoulder and neckline edge of the right front, trim the muslin rectangle as shown. Label, using a pencil and marking very lightly.

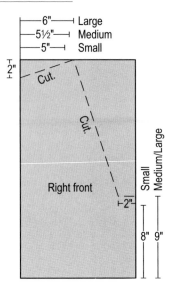

2. To shape the shoulder and neckline edge of the left front, trim the muslin rectangle; label as shown.

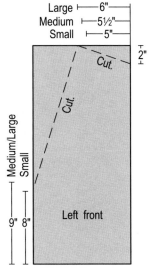

3. To shape the shoulders of the back fabric and the muslin piece, fold each rectangle in half lengthwise and cut the angle as shown. Label the muslin back.

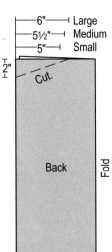

4. Cover the front muslin pieces with crazy patchwork as described in "The Crazy Patchwork Method" on pages 10–14. Begin with the five-sided patch in the widest section of each front piece as shown. If you wish to crazy patch the sides and back pieces, begin with the five-sided patch in the center of each piece.

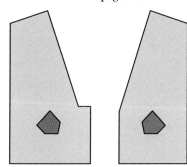

Right front   Left front

5. Embroider all patchwork as desired. If you did crazy patchwork on the sides and back, keep the embroidery simple as described in Embroidery Tip #8 on page 72. If you did not embroider the back and side panels, machine baste the matching muslin piece to the wrong side of each piece in order to balance the back with the heavier, embellished fronts.

6. Sew the front and back panels together at the shoulders. Press the seams open.

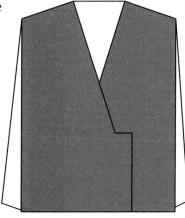

Sew shoulder seams.

7. With bottom edges even, sew a side piece to each side back edge. Press the seams open.

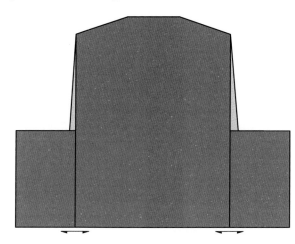

8. With bottom edges even, sew each side piece to each side front edge. Press the seams open.

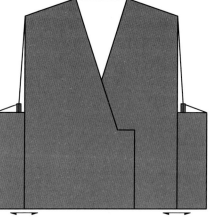

Lining Construction and Finishing

1. *With wrong side up*, cut the shoulder angle and neckline edge on the front lining pieces as shown in steps 1 and 2 of "Vest Construction" on page 56.

2. With right sides together, fold the back lining piece in half lengthwise and cut the shoulder angle as shown in step 3.

3. Sew the front and back linings together at the shoulders. Press the seams open.

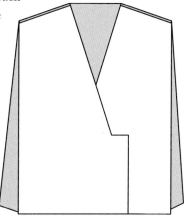

Sew shoulder seams.

4. Sew the side lining pieces to the side front and side back edges. Press the seams open.

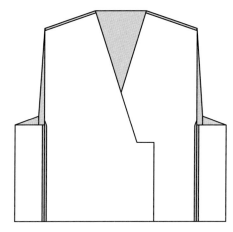

5. Place the vest and lining together with wrong sides facing and raw edges even. Pin-baste around the back and front neckline edges as shown.

6. Measure 1" from the neckline edge at the center back and draw a shallow curve that tapers back to nothing at the shoulder seams. Cut on the drawn line through both layers, being careful to avoid the pins. Unpin and remove the lining from the vest.

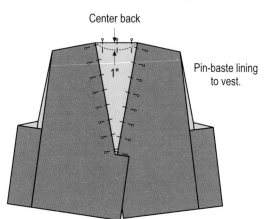

Center back

1"

Pin-baste lining to vest.

7. With the machine set for 15 to 18 stitches per inch, staystitch ¼" from the raw edge of the inside corner of the right vest front and right vest front lining, pivoting at the corner.

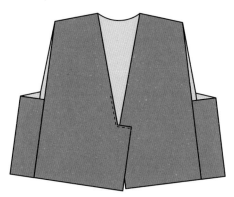

Staystitch ¼" from raw edges at inside corner.

8. Sew or fuse interfacing to the wrong side of the neckband. With right sides together, stitch the 2 neckband pieces together as shown and press the seam open.

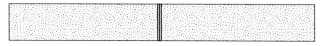

9. With wrong sides together, fold the neckband in half length-wise and press lightly.

10. With right sides together and raw edges even, pin the neckband to the vest neckline, placing the seam at the center back. *Note that the neckband is longer than necessary at both ends.* Stitch ¼" from the raw edges, beginning and ending the

stitching at the seam intersections of the right front and left front neckline edges as shown.

11. On the inside, clip to the stitching at the inner corner of the right front neckline. Do not clip the neckband layer.

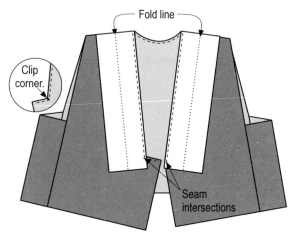

Fold line

Clip corner.

Seam intersections

Staystitch ¼" from raw edge.

12. With right sides together, fold the ends of the neckband back onto themselves along the fold line, raw edges even. Stitch across the ends, ending the stitching at the neckband seam line as shown. Trim the neckband ends ⅛" to ¼" from the stitching. Clip the corners. Turn the neckband right side out and press.

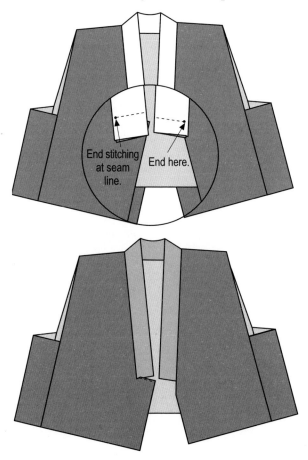

End stitching at seam line.

End here.

13. Baste the raw edges of the neckband and vest together.

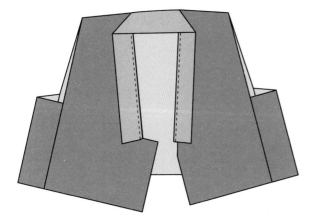

14. With right sides together, pin the lining to the neckline edge of the vest. Stitch ¼" from the raw edge. On the right front where the collar ends, clip the lining seam allowance to, but not through, the seam line.

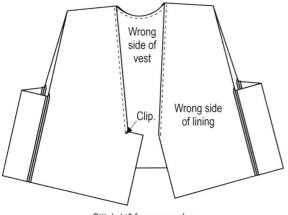

Wrong side of vest

Clip.

Wrong side of lining

Stitch ¼" from raw edge.

15. Turn the vest right side out and press the neckline edge. Baste the layers together ¼" from all raw edges.

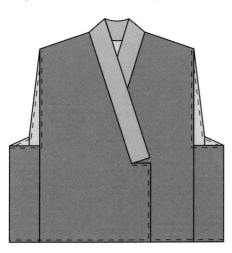

Baste all layers.

16. Make 3 button tabs as described on page 16. Pin or baste the tabs to the right side of the right front edge, positioning the first tab 1" below the top edge. Space the remaining tabs 3" apart.

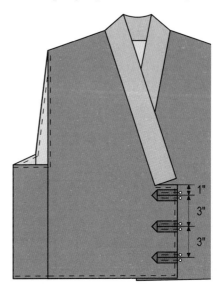

1"

3"

3"

17. Cut binding strips 1¼" wide and bind all raw edges as described in "Binding" on page 17.

18. Lap the right front 2½" on top of the inner edge of the left front. Sew buttons in place under the tabs.

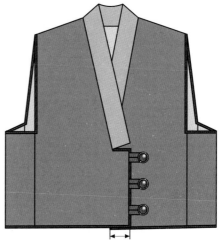

2½"

Scrappy Vest

This vest is made of small squares, the perfect background for your favorite scraps. A kimono-style neckband ties all your fabric choices together. You may cut the back and side panels from a single fabric for a different look. Make it sophisticated in silk and lace, or do a more down-to-earth version in cotton scraps. It's up to you.

Tutti Frutti à la Rutti by Deborah Brunner, 1995, Sarasota, Florida. I must have been influenced by my new surroundings when I made this vibrant vest. The bright citrus-colored silks I chose to go with the fairly tame cotton brocade that inspired this project remind me of luscious scoops of sherbet. The vest is a celebration of my first year in Florida.

Shimbumi by Deborah Brunner, 1995, Sarasota, Florida. Machine-embroidered vines with hand-embroidered silk-ribbon flowers add dimension to the patchwork of Japanese cottons in this version of the Scrappy Vest. I cut the back and sides from a single Japanese print and borrowed the neckband style from the Himalayan Jacket shown on page 41.

Materials

In addition to assorted fabrics totaling approximately 1¼ to 1½ yards for the crazy patchwork, you will need the following materials:

	Small	Medium	Large
Muslin	⅝ yd.	¾ yd.	1⅛ yds.
Lining	⅝ yd.	¾ yd.	1⅛ yds.
Neckband	¼ yd.	¼ yd.	¼ yd.
Interfacing	¾ yd.	⅞ yd.	1 yd.

Cutting

Fabric	No. of Pieces	Small	Medium	Large
Muslin	24	5½" x 5½"	6½" x 6½"	7½" x 7½"
Neckband*	2	4½" x 24½"	4½" x 28½"	4½" x 34½"
Interfacing*	2	4½" x 24½"	4½" x 28½"	4½" x 34½"*
Lining, back	1	15½" x 20½"	18½" x 24½"	21½" x 28½"
Lining, front	2	5½" x 20½"	6½" x 24 ½"	7½" x 28½"
Lining, sides	2	5½" x 10½"	6½" x 12½"	7½" x 14½"

The neckband and neckband interfacing pieces are cut a little long; you will trim them later.

Vest Construction

Use ¼"-wide seam allowances unless otherwise noted.

1. To shape the shoulders, trim 4 of the muslin squares as shown. Use rotary-cutting equipment to cut straight lines.

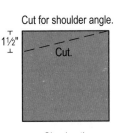

Cut for shoulder angle.

1½"

Cut.

Shaping the shoulder angle

2. Arrange the shaped pieces and label them as shown, using a pencil and marking very lightly.

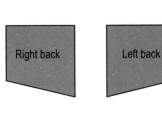

Right back

Left back

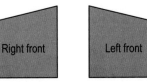

Right front

Left front

3. Cover all muslin pieces with crazy patchwork as described in "The Crazy Patchwork Method" on pages 10–14. Begin with the five-sided patch in the center of each muslin piece and work on the marked side of each shaped piece. Embroider as desired. See the "Hand Embroidery Stitch Guide" on pages 73–80.

Crazy-patched square

4. Arrange the pieces for each front in the desired order, with shaped shoulder pieces at the top. Sew the pieces together for each front; press the seams open.

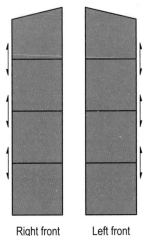

Right front   Left front

5. Arrange and sew the back pieces together in 3 vertical rows. Press the seams open. Sew the completed rows together and press the seams open.

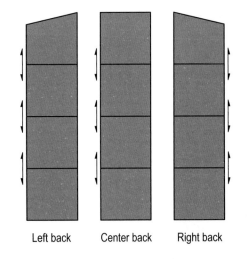

Left back   Center back   Right back

6. Use the remaining 4 squares for the side panels. Sew the pieces together as shown; press the seams open.

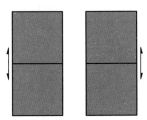

Side panels

7. Sew the side panels to the back panel and press the seams open. With right sides together, sew the front and back panels together at the shoulders. Press the seams open.

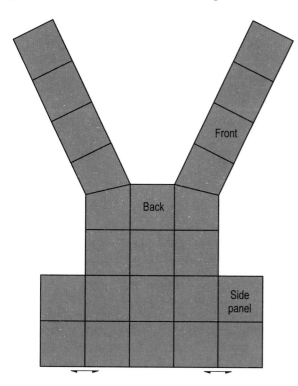

Lining Construction and Finishing

1. Layer the lining front panels, *wrong sides together*, and fold the back panel in half lengthwise, *wrong sides together* with raw edges even. Cut the shoulder angles.

1½" ⌶ — Cut.
1½" ⌶ — Cut.

Fold

Front lining
Cut 2.

Back lining
Cut 2.

2. Sew the side linings to the back lining and press the seams open. Sew the front linings to the back lining at the shoulders and press the seams open.

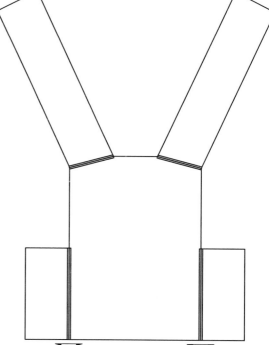

3. With right sides together, stitch the lining to the vest as shown, ending the stitching on the front panels at the appropriate point for the size you are making. Clip to, but not through, the stitching at the inside corners on the vest back. Turn the vest right side out and press the stitched edges carefully.

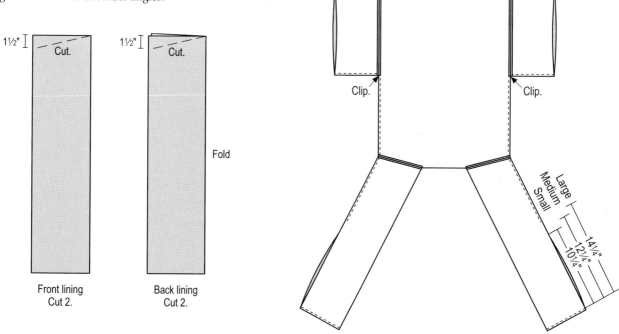

Clip.
Clip.

Large
Medium
Small

14¼"
12¼"
10¼"

4. Measure 1" from the neckline edge at the center back and draw a shallow curve that tapers back to nothing at the shoulder seams. Cut on the drawn line.

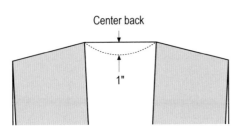

Center back

1"

5. With the right side of the vest facing you and the bottom edge of the back closest to you, fold the front down and tuck the side panel into the opening at the front side seam between the lining and the vest. Stitch through all layers, backstitching at the beginning and end of the seam. Repeat with the remaining front.

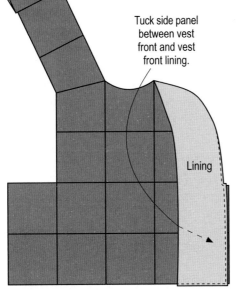

Tuck side panel between vest front and vest front lining.

Lining

6. Sew or fuse the interfacing to the wrong side of the neckband. With right sides together, stitch the 2 neckband pieces together at the center back and press the seam open. Turn under and press ¼" along one long edge of the neckband.

Turn under ¼".

7. With right sides together and long raw edges even, pin the neckband to the right side of the vest, matching the neckband seam and the center back. The band will extend below the bottom edge of the vest fronts. Stitch ¼" from the raw edge.

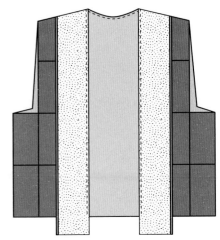

8. Turn the band to the inside, placing the turned and pressed edge along the stitching; press carefully.

9. Open the band and turn it back onto itself, right sides together. Stitch across the bottom edge a scant ¹⁄₁₆" below the bottom edge of the vest. (This allows the thickness of the patchwork to fit inside the band smoothly when turned.) Trim the excess band below the stitching, leaving a ⅛"- to ¼"- wide seam allowance. Clip the corner.

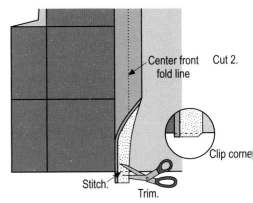

Center front fold line   Cut 2.

Clip corner

Stitch.   Trim.

10. Turn the band to the inside and slipstitch in place.

Slipstitch band to lining along seam line.

Creative Option: The band on the "Shimbumi" variation of this vest (page 61) is shorter than the finished vest and was added after binding the front edge with contrasting fabric.

To imitate this look:

1. Follow the cutting chart, but do not cut the neckband and interfacing yet.

2. Do the crazy patchwork and assemble the vest as shown in steps 1–7 of "Vest Construction" on pages 62–63.

3. Complete steps 1–5 of "Lining Construction and Finishing." Cut 2 neckbands and 2 neckband interfacing pieces, each 4½" wide and 1¼" shorter than the length from the center back to the front bottom edge of the vest. Apply the interfacing to the wrong side of the band pieces and sew together as shown in step 6 on page 64. Press the seam open. *Do not turn under one long edge.*

4. Fold the band in half lengthwise and stitch across the short ends ¼" from the raw edges. Clip the corners. Turn right side out and press.

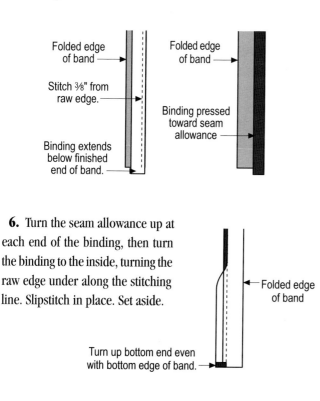

5. From contrasting fabric, cut a binding strip 1½" wide and the length of the neckband plus ½" for seam allowances. With right sides together and raw edges even, stitch the binding strip to the raw edge of the band, using a ⅜"-wide seam allowance. Press the binding toward the seam allowance.

Folded edge of band →

Folded edge of band →

Stitch ⅜" from raw edge. →

Binding pressed toward seam allowance →

Binding extends below finished end of band. →

6. Turn the seam allowance up at each end of the binding, then turn the binding to the inside, turning the raw edge under along the stitching line. Slipstitch in place. Set aside.

← Folded edge of band

Turn up bottom end even with bottom edge of band. →

7. To bind the front and back neckline edges, cut 2 strips, each 1¼" x 40", from contrasting fabric. Sew the 2 strips together as shown in step 1 of "Binding" on page 17. (The finished strip will be longer than you actually need.)

8. Bind the front edge and back neckline of the vest as you did the neckband (steps 5 and 6).

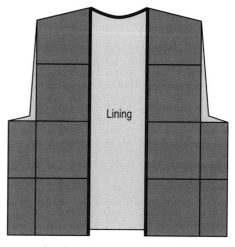

Lining

Bind front and back neckline edges.

9. Matching the neckband seam and the center back, tuck the bound edge of the neckband just inside the bound edge of the vest. Baste in place, then stitch in-the-ditch along the binding on the right side of the vest.

Binding on inner edge of band

Stitch in-the-ditch.

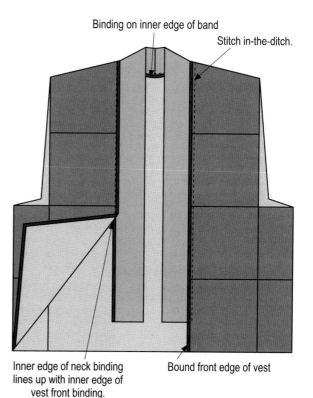

Inner edge of neck binding lines up with inner edge of vest front binding.

Bound front edge of vest

Using Commercial Patterns for Crazy-Patched Garments

Blue on Blue Fantasy by Melody Naskale, 1995, North Port, Florida. This traditional, baseball-style jacket from a commercial pattern was made with hand-dyed cotton fabrics. The background stitching was done by machine, and Melody added embroidered silk ribbon and appliquéd lace motifs for more texture and visual interest.

Katy's Classic Collage by Beth and Katy Donaldson, 1995, Lansing, Michigan. Katy, a fourteen-year-old, loves fabrics with moon-and-star motifs. Her mother, Beth, created the patchwork using the fabrics Katy chose, then Katy did all the beading and added the charms. Beth helped with the embroidery and finished the vest, which she made from a favorite commercial pattern. Be sure to look for the giraffes hidden among the patches.

Happy Birthday Rhonda by Deborah Brunner, 1995, Sarasota, Florida. This vest, made from a commercial pattern, was stitched for my friend Rhonda Anderson's "thirtysomething" birthday. The gold, purple, and green fabrics were meant just for her. I used a variety of threads and ribbons for the embroidery. Notice how the embellishment helps blend and blur the seam lines between patches.

Colleen's Concerto by Beth and Colleen Donaldson, Lansing, Michigan. Colleen, a twelve-year-old, chose the fabric, charms, and buttons for this vest. As the musician in the family and a collector of elephants, Colleen chose charms that reflected her passions. Her mother, Beth, did the patchwork, embroidery, and finishing on this longer style made from a commercial pattern.

Thai Nights *by Diedra Garlock, 1995, Lansing, Michigan. Patchwork, in a combination of primary colors and dark fabrics, creates a bold statement for this colorful vest, which Diedra made from a commercial pattern. Embellishments include silk-ribbon work and beading.*

Beginner's Luck *by Karen Mirras, 1995, Okemos, Michigan. Karen used a combination of complementary blue and russet fabrics to create this wonderful vest, adorned with a variety of buttons and beadwork along with rich embroidery. The vest was made from a commercial pattern.*

The basic crazy patchwork method described on pages 10-14 can also be used to create garments using commercially available patterns. Before selecting a pattern, be sure to read the guidelines in this section.

Vest Pattern Selection and Patching

• A very fitted vest pattern is difficult to crazy patch unless it has a princess seam line that runs from the shoulder seam to the bottom edge of the vest. Crazy patch each complete vest section *before* sewing the fronts together, then add the embroidery.

For a fitted vest, choose a pattern
with a princess seam line.

• Patterns with a shallow bust dart are easily crazy patched. Avoid patterns with deep darts. Sew the dart in the muslin base *before* you do the crazy patching. You will lose some of the shaping provided by the darts, so if you are full-busted, look for a vest pattern without darts.

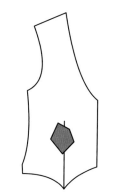

Make the dart in the muslin base before doing the crazy patchwork.

• Cover the muslin pieces with crazy patchwork as described on pages 10–14. Begin with the five-sided patch in the center of the largest section of the vest front as shown.

• As you reach the shoulder area of your vest foundation, you must still make three cuts, the two straight cuts and the angled cut as described on pages 10–14. This will create two new places to add fabric patches to prevent undesirable stripes from forming.

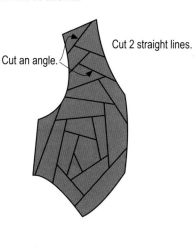

Cut an angle.

Cut 2 straight lines.

Jacket Pattern Selection and Patching

• Select a simple pattern that has separate front, back, and sleeve pattern pieces. Patterns with more than four basic pieces, including a collar, are not suitable. Refer to the discussion about vest pattern selection.

• The crazy patchwork method described in this book was designed for garments constructed after the individual pieces have been covered with patchwork. Follow the basic directions for crazy patchwork as described on pages 10–14, beginning with the five-sided patch in the center of the largest section of each piece, as shown.

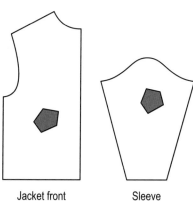

Jacket front   Sleeve

• Because jacket pattern pieces are often considerably larger than vest pattern pieces, the crazy patches will become larger and larger as you reach the outer edges. If you cannot resist trying the method on a pattern with cut-on sleeves, you will need to work carefully and patiently to create a visually pleasing patchwork composition. Begin with the five-sided patch in the center of the largest section of the jacket piece, then work outward in a fashion similar to the one shown below. As you reach the edges of the vest or jacket foundation, you must still cut the two straight sides and an angle on each added piece as described on pages 11–12. This will prevent the formation of stripes rather than a patchwork effect.

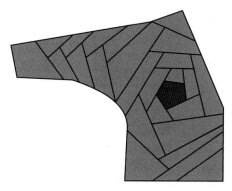

Jacket front with cut-on sleeve

• Embroider the jacket pieces as desired. Use simpler embroidery and embellishment on crazy-patched sleeves and back pieces. Refer to Embroidery Tip #8 on page 72.

General Directions

1. Cut from muslin all garment pieces that you wish to crazy patch. To purchase the muslin, refer to the garment yardage requirements on the pattern envelope.

2. Yardage for the crazy patchwork will vary depending on the pattern. In general, add approximately ¼ to ½ yard to the garment yardage for a vest. You may need an additional ¾ to 1 yard for a jacket.

3. Cover the muslin pieces with crazy patchwork and embroider as desired. If you crazy patched the sleeves or back of a garment, refer to Embroidery Tip #8 on page 72 before you begin your embroidery.

4. Assemble the garment, following the directions on the pattern guide sheet.

Embroidery and Embellishment

Embroidery and other embellishments provide the "icing on the cake" of crazy patchwork. The stitches and the threads and ribbons you use make up a large part of your individual style. Beads, buttons, and charms add sparkle to the finished garment.

EMBROIDERY

I have favorite embroidery threads and stitches that I seem to use again and again. They have become my trademark, and people recognize my work because of them. You may find this happens to you as you experiment with stitches and threads. If you really love something, it bears repeating.

The embroidery stitches in this section can be done with a variety of threads and ribbons. The vast number available is bound to spur your creativity to new heights. Try your stitches using any of the ribbons and threads listed below as well as others you discover in visits to your favorite fabric and thread haunts. Traditional embroidery stitches can take on an entirely new look simply by changing the thread or ribbon, so don't be afraid to experiment. Browse in your local needlework shops and try some of the threads used for needlepoint and crewel embroidery too. They may add just the effect you've been trying to achieve.

Ribbons and Threads

Silk Ribbon: Silk ribbon is my favorite stitching medium. Silk-ribbon embroidery has become very popular over the past few years. The ribbon is available in a wide range of colors, including beautiful hand-dyed versions. The most commonly used widths are 2mm, 4mm, and 7mm. These are suitable for embroidered flowers, leaves, and stems. Traditional embroidery stitches take on a fabulous dimension when stitched with silk ribbon.

Silk Buttonhole Twist: This lustrous thread makes wonderful stems and stamens.

Rayon Threads: Among the many rayon threads available are Brazilian embroidery threads, Marlitt, and several threads designed for machine embroidery. These threads are ideal for flowers, stems, and stamens as well as for traditional stitch combinations.

Perle Cotton: Look for this mercerized cotton thread in sizes 8 and 12. It can be used as you would use rayon thread and silk buttonhole twist.

Silk Floss: This soft, lustrous thread is usually available in small skeins that can be divided into six to twelve strands. Use it to make beautiful stems and flowers. Try using it for traditional stitch combinations with multiple colors. Hand-dyed varieties are also available.

Art Silk: This is a very shiny, very fine silk thread, usually packaged in six-strand skeins. Use all six strands for traditional embroidery stitches; divide to use for fine stamens.

Ribbon Floss: Use this flat woven rayon for flowers, leaves, stems, and traditional stitches. It has a high luster, adding a nice sheen to your work.

Metallic Threads: These are available in a number of sizes; the finer ones work very well for embroidery. Try using them as an overlay or accent, such as shadowing a traditional embroidery stitch. The heavier metallics may be couched into place.

Tools

You will need a few basic supplies to begin your embroidery.

Needles: For silk-ribbon embroidery, you will need chenille needles. Size 18 is the most versatile size. It will take a 7mm-wide silk ribbon through fabric with the least wear and tear and is suitable for use with most other embroidery thread you might use. Choose size 20 and 22 chenille needles for finer threads such as buttonhole twist, Brazilian rayon, and perle cotton. Crewel needles, sizes 8 and 9, are perfect for fine threads such as art silk and fine metallics.

Scissors: You will need a pair of 3"- to 4"-long, sharp-pointed scissors for snipping threads and ribbon.

Laying Tool: Use this straight, smooth tool to help manipulate silk ribbon. A plastic yarn needle works well for this task.

Pincushion: Use this as a place to store your needles when not in use.

Storage: I use translucent plastic boxes divided into compartments to store my embroidery supplies. Some of these boxes have adjustable compartments. Since I take my embroidery on the road, these boxes allow portability. I stack them all in a large basket and I'm ready to go. When I want to travel light, I choose the items I need for a specific project and organize them in a single box.

Stitching Tips

The following tips will help make your embroidery experience a successful and happy one.

Tip #1:

When using silk ribbon, use a 12" to 14" length. The ribbon will wear too much if you cut it any longer, and you won't be able to use the entire length. Tie a traditional knot at one end of the ribbon and attach the other end to the needle with a small stitch as shown.

Ribbon anchored on needle

Tip #2:

When using silk ribbon, stitch with a loose tension to maintain dimension in the finished stitches. You may also manipulate the ribbon for various stitches to keep it flat. Use a large plastic yarn needle for this manipulation. Do not use the end of your needle for this purpose, as it may cause runs or snags in the silk. End your stitching with a knot, or stitch the tail to another piece of ribbon on the back of your work.

When you tie the knot, before you tighten it down, insert the needle into the loop and place the point of the needle on the place where the ribbon came through the fabric. This holds the stitch in place on the front. Use regular sewing thread if you stitch the tails in place. I keep a small needle with neutral thread in my pincushion for this job.

Ending ribbon

Pull on ribbon attached to eye of needle.

Tip #3:

Cut rayon or silk threads 18" long. This is a manageable length to control twisting. If your thread begins to twist back on itself while you are stitching, drop your needle so it dangles at the end of the thread. The thread will untwist itself; then you can resume stitching. Use this method for metallic threads as well.

Tip #4:

A traditional knot often comes undone in rayon or silk thread. Instead, use the quilter's knot, with one or two twists.

Wrap thread around needle.

Pull.

Hold wraps firmly with thumb and forefinger. Pull needle, letting wraps slide to the end of the thread.

Take two small backstitches to secure the thread rather than tying a knot when you are ready to end the stitching. Split the thread where it entered the back of your work as you take the backstitch.

Tip #5:

Do not use an embroidery hoop. The muslin base of the crazy patchwork provides enough stability to embroider, and a hoop might crush or distort previous stitches and your ribbon work.

Tip #6:

Stitch in a meandering fashion over the seam lines. This technique provides more interest with several of the stitches. See "Crazy Cache Embroidery Pattern" on page 84.

Tip #7:

Keep all stitching and beading inside the ¼"-wide seam allowances (or ⅝"-wide in commercial patterns) so it won't interfere with the garment construction.

Tip #8:

Do not use dimensional silk-ribbon embroidery on the back or sleeves of your garments. These areas receive a lot of wear and tear. If these areas have crazy patchwork, use a simple flat stitch, such as a feather or buttonhole stitch, over the seams instead.

Tip #9:

Before you embroider designs on the chest area of a garment, check the placement. In front of a mirror, hold the piece up against your body and pin or mark the best place. Ditto for the dangling charms.

Hand Embroidery Stitch Guide

You can use the following stitches individually along a seam line or in any number of interesting combinations.

Refer to the closeup color photos in the project section of this book to see them on actual garments. Additional combinations appear on page 80. I'm sure you will come up with a few of your own. When a stitch can be done in traditional thread *and* silk ribbon, both versions appear in the photos.

Feather Stitch

This stitch is a wonderful filler stitch. Use it by itself in a meandering fashion along seams, or add French knots or beads to the little branches that characterize the stitch.

1. Bring the needle up at A, then down at B, forming a U-shape.

2. Bring the needle back up at C to form the "catch," then down at D, once again forming a U-shape.

3. Bring the needle back up at E to catch the U. Continue working to the left and right in this manner.

4. Connect multiple stems at a "branch."

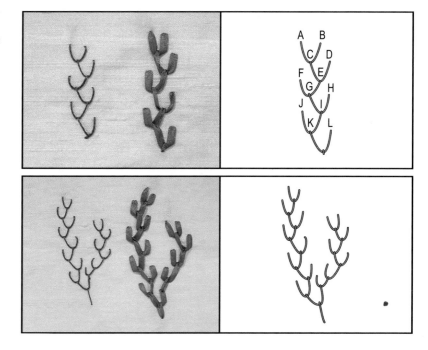

Stem Stitch

Just as the name indicates, you can attach flowers and leaves to this stitch. Meander the stem stitch over a seam as a vine or branches. For stems, you may use silk ribbon as well as any of the other materials listed in "Ribbons and Threads" on page 71.

1. Bring the needle up at A, then down at B to create a short stitch (⅛" to ³⁄₁₆" long with embroidery threads or ¼" to ⅜" long with 2mm or 4mm silk ribbon).

2. Bring the needle up at C, just in front of A. Repeat to form a stem. For a smooth stem, keep the thread above or below the stitch line for the entire length of the stem; do not alternate sides or you will have a lumpy stem.

3. To blend stems, stitch very close to previous stem.

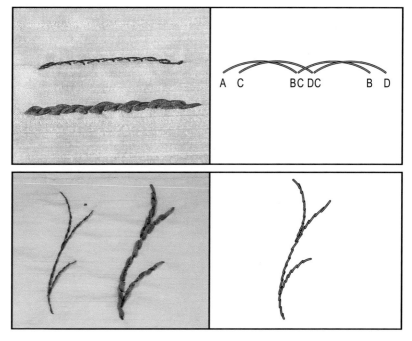

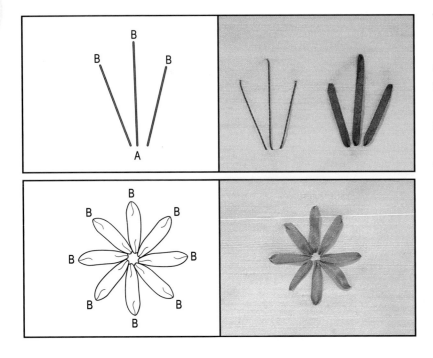

Straight Stitch

Use this simple stitch to make flower petals with silk ribbon, and stems and stamens with various other threads.

1. Bring the needle up at A, then down at B. Repeat for each stem or stamen.

2. To make flower petals, take straight stitches in a circle, using silk ribbon.

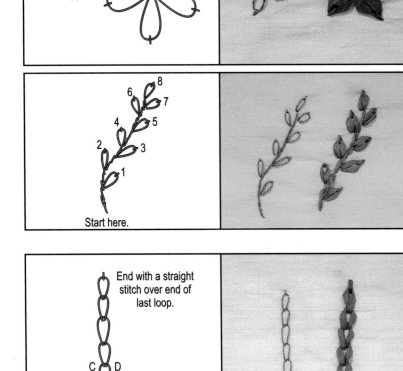

Detached Chain or Lazy Daisy Stitch

Use this stitch to make flowers or leaves with just a change of thread or ribbon color.

For flowers:

1. Bring the needle up at A, then down at B, forming a U-shaped loop.

2. Bring the needle up at C, then down at D to form a catch stitch over the loop. Repeat the stitch in a circular fashion to form a flower.

For leaves along a stem:

Begin at the base of a stem and work back and forth up both sides to form leaves.

Chain Stitch

Use the chain stitch to make stems, long leaves, and flower stalks. Different threads and ribbons in various colors create varied effects. Experiment.

1. Bring the needle up at A, then down at B, forming a U-shape.

2. Bring the needle up at C inside the loop, then down at D to form the catch stitch and continue the chain. End with a straight stitch over the end of the last loop.

French Knot

Use the French knot to make flower centers with embroidery thread, taking 1 to 3 wraps around the needle, depending on how full you want the knot. Make 1 to 3 wraps with 2mm- or 4mm-wide silk ribbon to make small buds or flowers. If you want to create cascading flowers, such as wisteria, or the look of blossoms tumbling over a ledge, use several wraps of ribbon.

Bring the needle up at A; wrap thread around the needle the desired number of times and, keeping tension on the wraps, go down at B, close to A, but not in the same hole.

When using silk ribbon, keep the wraps soft around the needle and let the ribbon twist. Do not use tension.

Ribbon Stitch

This is a very versatile stitch made with 4mm- or 7mm-wide silk ribbon. With a change of ribbon color, you can make a flower petal and a leaf.

1. Bring the needle up at A; smooth the ribbon and leaving a little slack, insert the needle at B. This is the end of the petal or leaf. Pull the ribbon through until the end rolls to a point and stop.

2. To make a flower, continue in a circle as shown.

3. To make leaves, add ribbon stitches to a stem, beginning at the base and working up alternating sides.

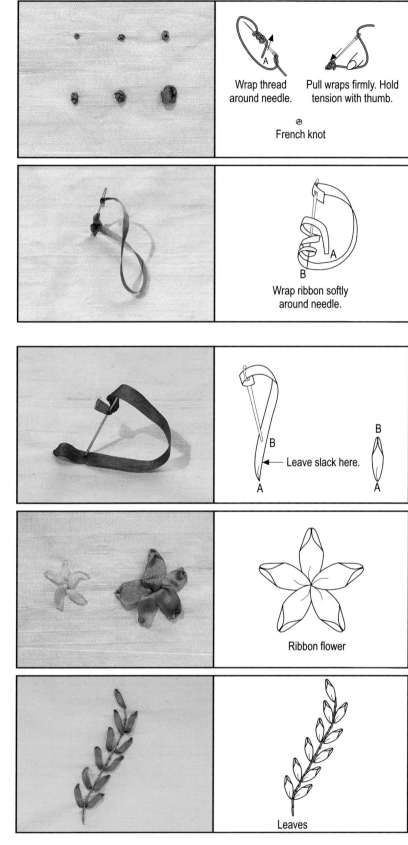

Wrap thread around needle.

Pull wraps firmly. Hold tension with thumb.

French knot

Wrap ribbon softly around needle.

Leave slack here.

Ribbon flower

Leaves

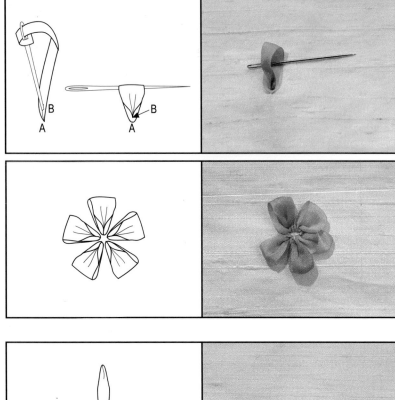

Looped Flower

This is a showy, dimensional flower you can do with either 4mm- or 7mm-wide silk ribbon. Use French knots or beads as stamens at the center to anchor each of the petals.

1. Bring the needle up at the flower center (A) and smooth out the ribbon. Insert the needle back into the ribbon very close to the center at B. Pull the loop that forms, keeping the ribbon flat. Use a laying tool, such as the large needle shown, to hold the loop until it is the desired length.

2. Bring the needle up again in a new hole and repeat. Continue making petals in this manner, usually 5 or 6, to complete the flower.

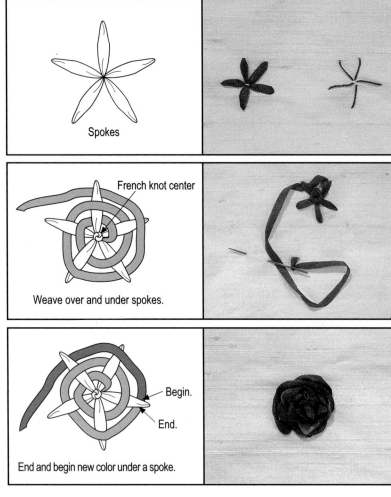

Spider Rose

This lovely rose adds dimension to silk-ribbon work. You can work the spokes with a thinner embroidery thread if you wish, but I prefer to use ribbon for the spokes as well as the filler. Use 4mm-wide ribbon. Try using 2 colors of ribbon or hand-dyed ribbon for a more natural look.

1. Make 5 spokes of the same length, spacing the straight stitches evenly in a circle.

2. Bring the needle up in the center of the spokes and make a French knot with 3 wraps around the needle. See "French Knot" on page 75.

3. Bring the needle back up in between 2 of the spokes next to the French knot. Begin to weave the ribbon over and under the spokes, using the eye of the needle to avoid catching the fabric underneath the spokes. Allow the ribbon to twist once between the spokes to form a petal. Do not pull the weaving tight, since you want the petal to be soft.

4. Weave until the spokes are filled. If you made one of the spokes a little long, it will show when the others do not. This is a good place to add a leaf. End by going down just beyond the last petal formed by going over a spoke. If you run out of ribbon before completing the rose or if you wish to add a new color, end and begin under a spoke.

Coral Stitch

This is a traditional embroidery stitch that can be worked along a seam or back and forth across a seam.

1. Bring the needle up at A. Lay the ribbon or thread in the direction you want the stitch to travel (left or right).

2. With the needle at an angle, go down at B and come up at C. Pull the ribbon through with the needle traveling over the ribbon loop that has formed. This creates a knot in the ribbon. Repeat for the desired length.

You can work this stitch back and forth over a seam and use irregular spacing if you wish.

You can use the stitch as a stem too. The knot in the stitch forms a calyx for flower petals. Extend the ribbon beyond the last knot and make a ribbon stitch to form a pointed tip as shown on page 75.

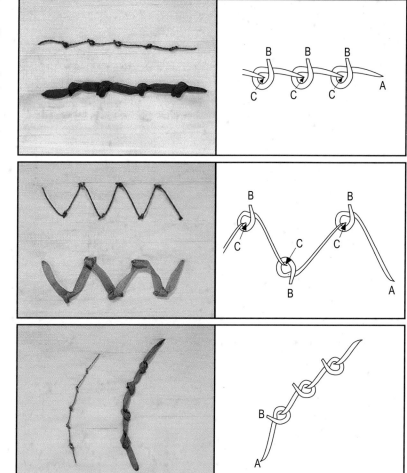

Couching Stitch

Use this stitch for threads and ribbons that will not pull through fabrics easily—bouclé and heavy metallic threads, for example. The heavy threads lie on top of the fabric, and a finer thread is used to hold them in place.

1. Thread a needle with a fine embroidery thread that matches or blends with the thread or ribbon you wish to couch in place.

2. Position the heavy thread or ribbon where you want it on the crazy patch. Bring the needle up at A, then cross the heavier thread and insert the needle at B, making a small stitch. Repeat along the length of the piece to be couched.

You can arrange a finer thread into a desired shape, such as a stem or flower, then couch in place with a piece of the same thread.

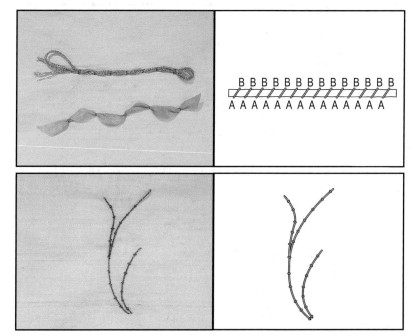

Buttonhole/Blanket Stitch

Work this simple stitch along a seam line or create meandering waves of varying heights for added interest.

1. Bring the needle up at A on the seam line. Go down at B, then up at C, crossing the needle over the thread.

2. Repeat by going down at B, then up at C. You can work this back and forth across a seam line at an angle.

Chevron Stitch

This stitch is worked back and forth over a seam. It is a good base for stitch combinations with threads and ribbon.

1. Bring the needle up at A. Cross the seam and go down at B, then up at C.

2. Bring the needle across B, then go down at D, creating a bar. Bring needle up under the bar at E, cross the seam, and go down at the next B. Repeat this progression to the end of the seam.

Cretan Stitch

This is another traditional embroidery stitch that looks equally good in traditional embroidery thread and in silk ribbon. Work the stitch back and forth across the crazy-patch seam. It is an excellent place to add dangling beads.

1. Bring the needle up on one side of the seam at A. Cross the seam, with the needle point perpendicular to the seam, then go down at B and come up at C.

2. Repeat by going down at B, then up at C on the opposite side of the seam.

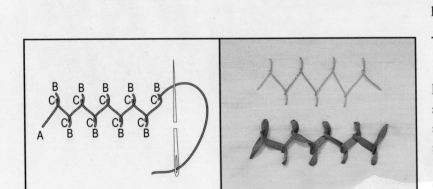

Herringbone Stitch

This stitch can be worked evenly back and forth over a seam or irregularly for textural interest.

1. Bring the needle up at A and cross the seam at an angle. With the needle held parallel to the seam and pointing toward A, take a small stitch from B to C.

2. Return to the opposite side of the seam line in the same manner. Continue to the end of the seam.

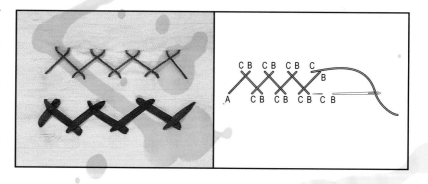

Fly Stitch

This stitch looks wonderful done in threads or silk ribbon and scattered over a crazy patch or a seam. Each stitch stands on its own.

Bring the needle up at A, down at B, up at C, then down at D.

Use several textures and colors of green thread to create the look of ferns.

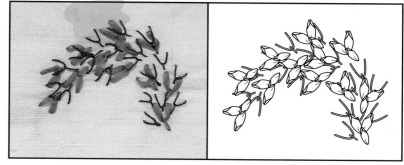

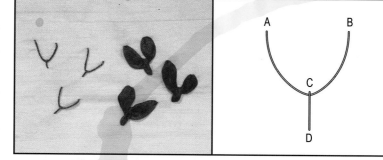

Bows and Streamers

Bows and streamers of silk and rayon ribbons add a wonderful dimension to crazy patchwork.

1. Fold the ribbon and pin in the desired shapes.

2. Anchor each twist or fold with a French knot or with a bead.

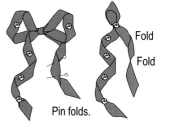

Stitch Combinations

Illustrated below are some of the myriad ways you can combine embroidery stitches to create designs.

Feather Stitch with French Knots

Ribbon Stitch Flowers

Chain Stitch Basket with Looped Flower

Lazy Daisy with Ribbon Stitch

French Knots Encircled with Chain Stitch

Couched Web and Coral Stitch Spider

Coral Stitch with Ribbon Stitch

Chain Stitch with Ribbon Stitch

Multi-twist French Knots

Machine Embroidery

This section is for those who do not have the time or the desire to hand embroider a vest or jacket. Since I love handwork so much, I had never really considered using machine embroidery on my crazy-patched garments. The mental image of straight rows of those static little figures so common on early zigzag machines was anything but inspiring! However, after I had spent some time teaching classes at a store that sold sewing machines, I realized that today's machines could do more than little zigzag figures and the scallop stitch! The women in the sewing-machine classes were doing wonderful things. When I saw the vine and flower designs, I wanted to explore combining them with more dimensional embroidery in my work.

Today's sewing machines are truly amazing. You can even connect some of them to your home computer, then create a design of your own or scan one you like from another source, and stitch it in no time. This kind of exciting technology opens new possibilities and timesaving machine-embroidery techniques that produce wonderful results. If you have limited time and a sewing machine with embroidery capabilities, you can still create fabulous one-of-a-kind garments.

Following are some guidelines and ideas for using machine embroidery on your crazy-patched garments.

❀ Consider machine embroidery as a replacement for the flat stitches—such as the feather or buttonhole stitch—on the high-wear areas of a garment. Machine-embroidery stitches will wear better and won't catch. They also won't get smashed if you sit on them (jacket back) or lean on them (sleeve elbows and forearms).

❀ If you use machine embroidery on the back and sleeves of a garment, you may embroider the front with dimensional silk ribbon work for showier effects. I used this technique on the Mandarin Coat (page 26). On one version of the Scrappy Vest (page 60), I used a Japanese fabric combined with black and turquoise and wanted something very simple that would not distract the eye from the patchwork pattern. A machine-embroidered flower-and-vine motif that undulated down the front panels, totally ignoring the crazy-patch seams, provided the solution. Silk ribbon–embroidered flowers following the pattern of the vines finished the design.

❀ Experiment with your machine and with a variety of threads to discover its capabilities. Select several different stitches and thread colors and do an entire project with the machine. There are many wonderful threads available for machine embroidery—some of them the same ones you can use for hand embroidery. Most shop owners are happy to discuss ideas and possibilities as well as demonstrate the threads they sell. On some machines, you may need to use a lighter-weight thread in the bobbin than you are using on top. Lingerie thread is a good choice for this purpose. It is a fine nylon thread by YLI Corporation and works very well with metallics and rayons. Check the instructions and suggestions for your individual machine.

❀ Many machine manufacturers recommend stabilizing fabric for embroidery. You can omit this step when embroidering crazy patches made with my method because the muslin base under the patches acts as the stabilizer.

❀ After selecting the embroidery motif and the threads you wish to use, stitch a sample. This step is very important. It's no fun to rip out machine-embroidery stitches, so take the time to test and adjust first. It's a good idea to make one or two extra crazy-patch squares, using the same fabrics you used for the garment, then do the following:

1. Thread your machine and insert a machine-embroidery needle in a size that will handle the thread you have chosen. Set the machine tension for embroidery. Check the owner's manual for your particular machine model.

2. Try the embroidery motif with the thread you have selected. Does it look the way you expected?

3. Does the design go over the seams without distorting? Some designs will hang up and jam when stitching over heavy seams. If stitch distortion is a problem, choose a different stitch and save this one to embellish the interior section of a patch.

❀ Keep your stitching samples in a notebook. Include both good and bad ones.

❀ If the embroidery thread breaks often, it may be twisting before it goes through the tension regulator on the machine. This is common with very slippery threads and metallics, which like to slide right off the spool and tangle. Try placing a serger net over the spool to hold the thread in place. Cut the mesh tube to fit your spool if necessary, or fold it in half over the spool.

I hope this information is enough to get you started. The best teacher is experience, so give yourself permission to experiment. You never know what might develop.

EMBELLISHMENTS

Embellishments are the miscellaneous items you add to your crazy patches in addition to the embroidery. They add a bit of glitz or a special look to your project. They can even be clues to your personality. Start collecting them now. Below you'll find a few possibilities.

Buttons: Old or new, there are many uses for buttons on a crazy-patch project besides the functional one. Plain white shirt buttons become flowers when sewn along an embroidered stem. Exotic shell buttons scattered on a crazy patch add a dash of pizzazz. Sewing simple buttons along a seam line, using colored thread and/or stitching in beads, adds textural interest. I have seen buttons for sale by the cupful in quilt shops—a good way to start a collection. If you love antique shops, you're sure to find button jars full of mundane as well as not-so-mundane treasures that can take on a new life in your work. Keep your eyes open!

Beads: Check the yellow pages for bead shops. Small seed beads make excellent replacements for French knots. Outline a seam line with bugle beads instead of stitching. Dangle Austrian crystals from the Cretan stitch for movement and interest. If you prefer natural materials, look for small animal and bird figures made of shell, bone, wood, and metal. Imagine a school of fish swimming across a crazy patch or a bird perched on a silk ribbon–embroidered branch. The possibilities are endless.

Other Jewelry: Don't forget to check your jewelry box; you never know what treasures you'll find there. Charms from a high school bracelet, beads from a broken necklace, and pins you don't wear are perfect candidates for enhancing your fancy work. Old rhinestone brooches look great on a crazy-patched garment and can be moved from one to another. If your jewelry box doesn't yield what you want, look for jewelry possibilities in secondhand and antique stores. Or check your local craft shop for brass charms. They're available in a wide array of sizes and motifs. Little Victorian flower baskets, birds, butterflies, and bees are perfect for crazy patches. They look wonderful sewn among the bouquets and floral sprays on the seams and patches of your garment.

Lace Trims: Look for these at your fabric store and check the sales table. Cotton and rayon trims can often be dyed to match the fabrics in your project. Antique stores are also a wonderful source for beautiful hand tatting, crocheted lace, and bits of vintage trim. These can be more costly but worth the price for a special garment.

Attach buttons, beads, and charms with Nymo™, a very strong, nylon monofilament thread made especially for beading. Look for it at bead and craft stores. It's available in several sizes; I recommend size D. Use with a size 9 crewel needle to attach buttons.

Beading Basics

Purchase size 10 beading needles. These are the largest and easiest to thread. A size 10 milliner's needle is also appropriate. It's a bit shorter than a beading needle and won't bend as easily.

1. Thread your needle with the Nymo and make a quilter's knot at one end, using 5 wraps around the needle to prevent the knot from pulling through the fabric.

2. Draw the needle through the fabric at the location for the first bead, pick up the bead with the point of the needle, and pierce the fabric with the needle very close to the spot where the needle came up.

3. Pull the thread snug. The bead should sit firmly in place. Continue to add beads in this manner, making a backstitch on the wrong side of the fabric after every fourth or fifth bead. This prevents the loss of many beads should you catch one and break the stitching.

4. If the next bead is more than ¾" away, take 2 or 3 backstitches to end the thread on the underside, reknot, and begin again.

5. Attach charms in the same manner. Some have a small ring you can stitch through. Others, such as animal and bird fetish beads, have a hole in their bodies.

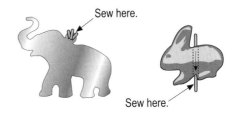

Sew here.

Sew here.

6. To attach larger beads and faceted glass crystals with your embroidery stitching, bring the needle up through the fabric and add 2 or 3 seed beads; then add the crystal, followed by one more seed bead. Return the needle through the crystal and the first seed beads; then go back into the fabric to the wrong side. The seed beads allow the crystal to dangle freely. Backstitch after adding each crystal/seed bead unit.

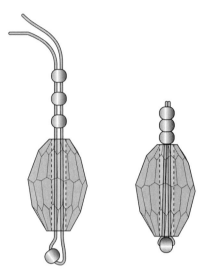

Button Basics

Attach flat buttons with a simple stitch through the holes, or do more decorative work by filling the centers with seed beads.

1. Using Nymo nylon thread, sew the button in place with several stitches, then bring the needle back to the surface through one of the holes.

2. Pick up the number of seed beads it takes to cross to the opposite hole, then take the needle down through the hole and pull the thread snug. Continue adding beads in this manner until the center is filled.

Helpful Hint

Attach dangling beads, buttons, and charms after completing the embroidery. If you sew them on before the embroidery is finished, your threads and ribbons will tangle and get caught as you stitch.

Lace and Trims

Add lace and other trims during the patching process so the cut ends get caught in a seam as you attach the next patches.

If you're not sure where you would like the trim, wait to add it until after the patching is completed and attach it by hand, turning under raw edges as needed. Add ribbon or thread embroidery over the edges to conceal any remaining loose ends.

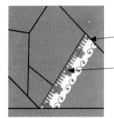

— Fold under and hand stitch ends.

— Embroider edge of trim.

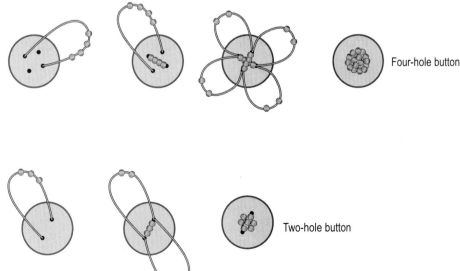

Four-hole button

Two-hole button

CRAZY CACHE EMBROIDERY PATTERN

Note

Template is 75% of actual size. For a full size, enlarge by 133% on a photocopy machine.

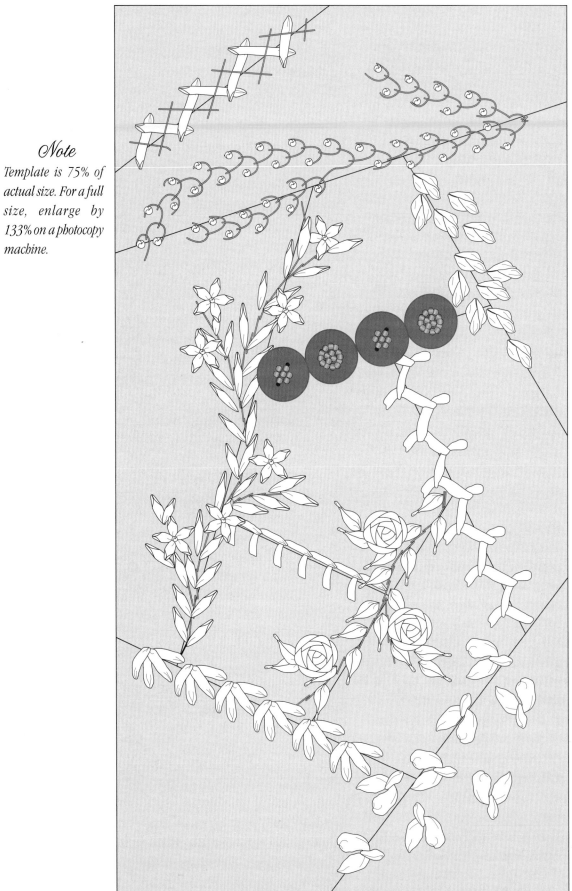

Meet the Author

Deborah Brunner shares her home in Sarasota, Florida, with her husband, Tom, and three "fabulous, talented cats." She was born and raised in the northern climes of Michigan, and her addiction to fabrics and fibers began when she was quite young. She learned to knit at age eight, using the little pink picks her mother used to hold hair rollers in place. Since then, Debbi has ventured into a number of fiber mediums, all of which have proved very satisfying.

A passion for beautiful clothing inspired Debbi to weave her own fabrics as well as to seek out the unusual and interesting. She has been sewing for thirty-five years and quilting for twelve, and still finds new things every day to add to her wearable art. She enjoys the search for lustrous threads, beautiful buttons, and wonderful charms and beads to use in embellishing her garments. She says that creating each garment using her treasures is a wonderful new adventure and a joy.

Sources

Couture Fabrics
1111 Swann Avenue
Old Hyde Park
Tampa, FL 33606
(813) 254-3112
Specializes in fine silk fabrics and laces.

D. J. Whimsy Beads Unlimited
6534 Gateway Avenue
Sarasota, FL 34231
(941) 925-9989
Beads from around the world, supplies, and books. Video catalog available. Wholesale and retail.

Elsie's Exquisiques
208 State Street
St. Joseph, MI 49085
(800) 742-SILK
Silk ribbon, threads, antique lace, and buttons.

Fabric Gallery
146 W. Grand River
Williamston, MI 48895
(517) 655-4573
Fine fabrics by mail.

Poplollies and Bellibones
(Lovely Maidens & Little Darlings)
2700 Eleventh Street Court
Moline, IL 61265
(309) 762-4951
Hand-dyed silk ribbon and threads. Wholesale only.

Quilter's Resource
PO Box 148850
Chicago, IL 60614
(800) 676-6543
Silk ribbon, threads, embroidery supplies. Wholesale only.

Sweet Child of Mine
139 E. Fremont Avenue
Sunnyvale, CA 94807
(408) 720-8426
Hand-dyed silk ribbon, art silks. Retail and wholesale.

YLI Corporation
482 N. Freedom Boulevard
Provo, UT 84601
(800) 854-1932
Silk ribbon, threads, machine-embroidery supplies. Wholesale and retail.

Bibliography

Books

Bond, Dorothy. *Crazy Quilt Stitches*. Cottage Grove, Oreg.: Dorothy Bond, 1981. This is a wonderful book of traditional embroidery stitches and combinations. The book is spiral bound for easy use.

Campbell-Harding, Valerie. *Bead Embroidery*. Berkeley, Calif.: Lacis Publications, 1993. This book explores a multitude of beading techniques for fabric and includes bead descriptions and uses.

Newhouse, Sue. *Creative Hand Embroidery*. Kent, England: Search Press Ltd., 1993. This book contains a wealth of information on thread embroidery, including dimensional embroidery for appliqué.

Magazines

The following magazines offer sources for fabric and embroidery supplies as well as inspiration and technical information:

Bead and Button
PO Box 56485
Boulder, CO 80323-6485

Inspirations
Country Bumpkin Publications
Box 194
Kent Town, South Australia 5071
Australia

Needle Arts
Embroiderer's Guild of America
EGA National Headquarters
335 W. Broadway, Suite 100
Louisville, KY 40202

PieceWork
Interweave Press
201 E. Fourth Street, DI-WP
Loveland, CO 80537

Threads
Taunton Press
PO Box 5506
Newtown, CT 06470-5506

Publications and Products

Many titles are available at your local quilt shop.
For more information, write for a free color catalog
to That Patchwork Place, Inc., PO Box 118, Bothell,
WA 98041-0118 USA.

☎ U.S. and Canada, call **1-800-426-3126** for the
name and location of the quilt shop nearest you.
Int'l: 1-206-483-3313   **Fax:** 1-206-486-7596
E-mail: info@patchwork.com
Web: www.patchwork.com   9.96